The End of Patriarchy

Self-birth, Totila Albert

THE END OF PATRIARCHY

And the Dawning of a Tri-une Society

Claudio Naranjo

Amber Lotus

Library of Congress Catalogue Card Number: 94-77707

Copyright © 1994 by Claudio Naranjo

All rights reserved. No part of this book may be reproduced in any form without the publisher's written permission.

For information, write to Amber Lotus, 1241 21st Street, Oakland, California 94607. Amber Lotus is a division of Dharma Enterprises.

Printed in USA by Dharma Enterprises

ISBN 1-56937-065-6

To the Memory of My Uncles,
Benjamin Cohen and Bruno Leuschner

It was Uncle Ben, my mother's elder brother, who suggested that I apply for the Fullbright Scholarship that brought me to the U.S. and indirectly out into the world. A medical student who became a journalist and then a diplomat, Ben Cohen was the United Nations' first Under Secretary General for public information and non-self-governing territories—at a time when the very existence of the UN hinged on its image. This book is to his *Encyclopedia of Nations* like the counterculture to the establishment, yet I think he would be pleased with my dedicating it to him.

Uncle Bruno was a marine engineer married to my mother's sister. At the end of his career he headed the United Nations' office for technical assistance for Latin America, and continued after his retirement to work toward an improvement of public affairs through personal research and writing articles for the newspapers. By the time of his death at the age of 92, he was seeking to persuade the Valparaiso authorities of the convenience of the building of a new highway for which he had worked out the costs and financing. It is particularly appropriate that I include him in the dedication of a book pervaded with the spirit of Totila Albert, since he was Totila's friend and regarded him (in his aggressive agnosticism) as some sort of saint. I think that he was one too, as may be conveyed by one of the last pieces of advice he gave me—still in the days of the Chilean military dictatorship: "we should pray," agnosticism notwithstanding, "that God enlightens our rulers—for it is very tempting to want them frying in oil."

CONTENTS

Preface by Reverend John Weaver	ix
FOREWORD On and For Our Times	xiii
CHAPTER I The Agony of the Patriarchal Order	1
CHAPTER II Educating the Whole Person for the Whole World	49
CHAPTER III A New Tool for the Reeducation of Love	75
CHAPTER IV A New Shamanism for Old Adam's Problems	101
Postlude by Manfred Max-Neef	141
Notes	149

PREFACE

Mankind faces two great opportunities during the next decade: one, the restoration of the environment, and, two, the cure of souls. Thomas Berry, in his book *The Dream of the Earth*, has dealt with the former while Claudio Naranjo, in his new book *The End of Patriarchy*, deals with the latter.

    I have known Dr. Claudio Naranjo for twenty-five years. What little I know about Sufism, the mystical side of Islam, I learned from him. Teilhard de Chardin has said, "research is the highest form of adoration." Claudio is chiefly a researcher of the Spirit. He stands still and silent yet in his quietness he goes deeper and deeper into the things of the Spirit. He has always been intercultural, interdisciplinary, and interreligious in his thinking and in his experience. A most competent medical doctor, a psychiatrist and a psychotherapist, yet far more deeply a shaman, a man seized by the Holy, the Numinous, the Mysterious Tremendum.

The issues he raises in this new book are between professionalism and spiritual awareness, between legalism and the movement of the spirit, between ritualism and spontaneity, between transcendence and immanence, between Apocalypse and Metamorphosis, and between the ordained priesthood and the seized shaman.

Pope John once said, "The Substance of the ancient deposit of the faith is one thing, and the way it is presented is another." Claudio, standing on the shoulders of Freud and Marx, has peripheral vision. He can look back with acute knowledge and understanding and he can look forward at "yon Distant light" with penetrating insight. His language is biodegradable and recyclable. He takes old words, old concepts and old ways of thinking and makes them fresh and new. If we are open to new truth, which in reality is primordial truth, we become enlightened. Whether we are termites consuming the earth or caterpillars whose metamorphosis will turn us into butterflies, we are human beings created in the image of God, endowed genetically with the potential of actualizing our true nature. This book contains a blueprint of those "imaginal cells" that can bring us to what Claudio calls "The Kingdom of the Three," Father, Mother, Child. As above, so below.

John Weaver, D.D., L.M., O.B.E., former Archdeacon of Grace Cathedral and retired Board Member of The U.S. Club of Rome Association

"Happy the man who reads this prophecy, and happy those who listen to him, if they treasure all that it says, because the Time is close."
>> THE BOOK OF REVELATION (1:3)

"But saving the world is not enough. We have to work to build an enlightened human society as well."
>> CHÖGYAM TRUNGPA[1]

ON AND FOR OUR TIMES

This book deals with four interrelated issues: social pathology, the "kingdom of God," collective transformation and neglected resources available to us at our time of crisis.

In regard to the root of the "macroproblem" besetting us, I propose that this is to be found—beyond partial answers such as technocracy, capitalism, rationalism, industrialism and so forth—in the obsolescence of something that has been intrinsic to all high civilizations from their beginning: the patriarchal organization of society and of the human mind.

In regard to the sane society—which, I believe, is our only alternative to self-annihilation—I propose that this can only be formed by emotionally healthy individuals, and that both intra-personal and interpersonal health lies in a loving balance in the relations between father, mother and child (in the family and within the individual's psyche).

Concerning the transformation that is taking place around us, I offer an optimistic interpretation—inasmuch as I view it as an integrative shift to prominence of the maternal and filial components of our being at a time of patriarchal crisis.

In regard to resources, I emphasize all that promotes the psychospiritual ripening of individuals, and focus mostly on the potential of a holistic education. In reviewing the resources available to a modern "education of the whole person for the whole world" I specially point out the special promise and relevance of a method that has still not been tried in schools: the so-called "Quadrinity Process."

Besides constituting essays that have to do with what happens both around and within ourselves at this moment (Chapters I and IV) or that deal with what we can do to speed up our individual and collective transformation (Chapters II and III), the four parts of the book may be called "holistic" essays in that they constitute variations on a single idea to the effect that the transformative change entails and is achieved through the reintegration of a threefoldness.

The expression of this threefoldness is differently viewed throughout them. In the first and third chapters, the theme is the threefoldness of "father," "mother" and "child," though in the first the emphasis lies in the social/cultural domain while in the third, "father," "mother" and "child" are those of the individual family and the inner psychodynamic domain. After having viewed human wholeness as a balance of sub-selves, family members and cultural values related to masculinity, femininity and childlikeness, wholeness is discussed in Chapter II as a balanced interplay between the intellectual, emotional and conative realms. The fact that in the second chapter I address the fourfold of body, feelings, intellect and spirit is no exception to the theme of threefoldness, for I do so in the context of an understanding of spirit as both unification and transcendence of the physical, affective and mental realms. (The relation of the three to the four may be understood in light of the metaphor of the three letters that constitute the fourfold name of God (Tetragramaton) in the Old Testament, or through the relation of the triangular base of a tetrahedron to its vertex.) The theme is tackled again in Chapter IV, on Neo-shamanism, where the emphasis is on the physiological threefoldness of the human brain. (From MacLean's expression, the "triune brain," I have derived that of a "tri-une society."[2])

It may be appropriate here to point out that in speaking of transformation I give this expression a meaning that goes beyond simple change. Already in speaking of individual transformation we mean not only change but a process of inner death and rebirth that has been known throughout time as a possibility of human beings (and which we may contemplate as an evolutionary potentiality intrinsic to our nature); also in reference to the collective realm, I prefer to reserve the term "transformation" (as distinct from "change") for something that might correspond to the known process of individual transformation: a collective evolution also entailing "death" and "rebirth" aspects. Obviously, in the realm of collective transformation the true fruit of the process is as yet unknown. It is noteworthy, in view of this conception, that even though the expression "collective transformation" is today becoming current, we tend to lose sight of the fact that—obvious as it may be that we are immersed in a process of deep transformation— we have not yet known a transformed community.

In his monumental study of history, Arnold Toynbee[3] clearly showed half a century ago how civilizations are collective organisms that are born and die, and he has illustrated how some of these have succumbed as a consequence of being overwhelmed by others. While we know this historical phenomenon of the birth and death of civilizations, we cannot say that we know a reborn civilization. The European Renaissance, which would deserve this name better than any other historical example, constitutes, when we consider it more closely, a new beginning (the beginning of a transformation in which we are still involved) and not the death/rebirth of a culture. In the same way in which we may say that our Western world was fathered by the Judeo-Christian culture and mothered by the Greco-Roman, we can say that the Renaissance was the time when out of these two streams there emerged a fruit that not only integrated them, but presented that individuality that we recognize as our own.

Just as the process of individual transformation—as we know it from the testimony of the spiritual traditions of the world—involves not one birth, but two (a birth of "water" and another of "spirit," a baptismal birth at the beginning of spiritual life and a baptism of fire that crowns its ending), we may also think that, in virtue of an isomorphism between the individual and the collective, the transformation of society may involve not only that first renaissance (our European Renaissance) but also the potential for that possible birth for which the Christian tradition reserves the word "resurrection."

Thus when I speak of transformation in the first and the last parts of this book, I do so from the implicit perspective that this is precisely what our time is about: for the first time in history we are propelled by a process of cultural death which is at the same time an incubation; and we put our hope in that this will be not merely a post-industrial period that we enter, but a condition that may differ essentially from what we have known during the course of our civilization—including classical civilizations in general.

It is often repeated today that our crisis is our great opportunity, and many are convinced that we are coming into a new age, "an Age of Aquarius," an age, which as Sri Aurobindo and Teilhard de Chardin anticipated, may constitute the supreme realization of our species. I share the thought of many in my belief that our only alternative to self-destruction is radical change and that we have limited time in which to bring it about. The essays that constitute this book have been formulated from this implicit context as contributions to the understanding of what happens in us and around us as well as what we could do from a position of conscious evolution to speed up our process.

As one who has been engaged more in teaching and lecturing than in writing in the past two decades, it is to be expected that what I write has been ripening through years of oral communication, and I feel grateful to the various audiences that have stimulated me to give shape to and refine my ideas.

My first account of Totila Albert's ideas (developed in Chapter I) was prompted in response to the invitation of the Association for Humanistic Psychology at the special annual meeting on the Bicentennial of the American Revolution.* The last, and most challenging in the spelling out of the content of this first chapter was an outdoor conference sponsored by the Santiago Gestalt Institute in Chile. Beyond the stimulus of the large audience that came together toward the end of that day in the courtyard of the "Centro El Arrayan," there was that of the special moment in local Chilean history: though General Pinochet continued to be in power, a plebiscite had demonstrated the country's preference for a return to democracy, and after the experiences of extreme left and extreme right, there was felt in Chile a wish and a hope for a new orientation. It was my awareness of the presence of a presidential candidate among the audience, and, more generally, the feeling that this audience was not just one of seekers (as have commonly been attracted to my talks throughout the years), but people likely to contribute to the future affairs of the country, which evoked

---

*Though I have often talked about the patriarchal problem, only once have my thoughts on this issue appeared in print—on occasion of a transcript of a dialog with Dr. Harman and D. Rudhyard—reproduced in *An Integral View,* published through the California Institute of Integral Studies.

the prescriptive tone of that talk—one in which I found myself not speaking to individuals alone, but to governments or more specifically to a possible "wise government." In the present book I continue to do the same—as Machiavelli when he wrote *The Prince,* though in opposite vein.

It is to the Association for Holistic Health and Education that I must give thanks for the invitation to continue thinking about education after the publication of *The One Quest*.[4] Since its 1981 conference in Santa Barbara I have become increasingly concerned with the urgency of educational reform, and have sought to influence the practice of education both at the local and international levels. Just as the second chapter of this book—on holistic education—develops a theme announced in the course of the first (on the obsolete patriarchal-mindedness), the content of the third (which deals with the Quadrinity Process) elaborates further on one of the educational resources to which I have wanted to call attention in what I write concerning a possible pedagogy of love. I have already said years ago, in the preface to Bob Hoffman's *No One is to Blame,*[5] that I felt a sort of John the Baptist to his work (in those days known as the Fischer-Hoffman Process). I happened to be the first to develop a group therapeutic application of his ideas and also the first to design an intensive form of the Process—something like the kernel of what today has become known in many countries of the world. I hope that this book may be a factor in interesting schools in exploring how the method can be applied to the education of teenagers.

I originally thought I would begin the book with what has ended up being its last chapter: an interpretation of our cultural movement as something centered in a new form of shamanism, and the idea that today's "sorcerer's apprentices" may constitute in a near future a critical human resource for the happy outcome of our transformation. When I talked about neo-shamanism for the first time, the term had not yet been used, but today we have witnessed a veritable explosion of interest in shamanism and many people in the West identify with the shamanic role. Now my use of the expression "new shamanism" is intended to point not so much at the imported shamanism of anthropologists and therapists who have become interested in learning from traditional shamans, but to a shamanism that is at the same time transcultural and Western: a nontraditional shamanism in which, I think, culminates the most typical aspect of the phenomenon: the primacy of individual creativity over tradition and the primacy of a transmission of consciousness itself—beyond the ideas, rituals and other *contents* of consciousness.

Though a number of books have appeared in recent years bearing on the subject of our "turning point" (to use Capra's felicitous expression),[6] I think this collection of essays emphasizing emotional rather than intellectual factors in the human transformation contains enough that is novel and enough potential inspiration to action that I feel both happy and hopeful in releasing it for publication.

May it be that this revised version of the subjects about which I have been talking for many years continues to stimulate initiatives that assist us in our crossing-over toward that "promised land" of soundness and fulfillment that we always wanted but that we have always sought in erroneous directions and through inappropriate means.

"The process by which scattered Neolithic villages became agricultural communities, then urban centers, and finally states has been called 'the urban revolution' or 'the rise of civilization.' It is a process which occurs at different times in different places throughout the world: first in the great river and coastal valleys of China, Mesopotamia, Egypt, India and Malaysia. Archaic states are everywhere characterized by the emergence of property classes and hierarchies; commodity production with a high degree of specialization and organized trade over distant regions; urbanism; the emergence and consolidation of military elites; kingship; the institutionalization of slavery."

....

"Slavery is the first institutionalized form of hierarchical dominance in human history; it is connected to the establishment of a market economy, hierarchies and the state."
GERDA LERNER[1]

"It will take a miracle to free the human mind: because the chains are magical in the first place. We are in bondage to authority outside ourselves . . ."
NORMAN O. BROWN[2]

"The first and perhaps most profound transition is due to the slow and reluctant but inevitable decline of patriarchy."
FRITJOF CAPRA[3]

THE AGONY OF THE PATRIARCHAL ORDER

1   The Problem-Complex

When, at the turn of the sixties, under the invitation of the Viking Esalen Publishing Program, I transformed my earlier technical report on human development resources—written for the Center for Educational Policy Research at SRI—into the book that was subsequently published as *The One Quest*,[4] I felt the need to preface the report itself with an observation of what I thought was taking place in the world: the death of a culture and the birth of another.

I wrote then inspired by what I saw taking place around me: I had arrived in California a few years earlier and felt there the effervescence which later came to be variously designated by such expressions as the "consciousness revolution," the "New Age," and the "human potential movement," among others. At that time I was more aware of the cultural *birth* or rebirth aspect than of the aspect of cultural *death* (although the latter was already visible particularly since Spengler published his book *The Decline of the West*[5]).

For someone arriving in California at the beginning of the sixties, most noteworthy was a kind of revolution—a "silent revolution"— which had stopped rebelling against things. It was a revolution so deep that it simply left behind certain values; more an inner than an outer revolution and yet so radical that it was appropriately described by Theodore Roszak[6] as the emergence of a "counterculture." It brought together people who, beyond the traditional dichotomy of right or left, turned their attention to their "own personal affairs." They began assuming a profoundly liberated attitude with regard to things and issues previously considered questionable—as much in the domain of widely accepted institutions as in the realm of ideologies. As a result of leaving behind the ready-made answers which they had readily accepted during their so-called "educational" process, in being left without answers, questions were born anew. I am not referring to intellectual questions, but principally to that question beyond words which lies behind many questions: existential longing, the quest. I would say that we are entering an age of seeking. A renaissance is taking place and just as the European Renaissance was centered around art, the renaissance of our times has centered around psychology and new religions.

As I have said, it was cultural rebirth that was most visible to me in the sixties. Now, however, the aspect of cultural death is easier to discern, and this is so because the crisis, with each day that passes, becomes more apparent.

I believe The Club of Rome was the first to raise the subject of this crisis. At least it was the first to make a decisive contribution in bringing about a more general worldwide awareness that everything which was being called progress entailed an imminent danger. The publication in the United States of the report entitled *The Limits to Growth*[7] warned us that if we continued to grow we would run the risk of becoming extinct like the dinosaurs. It went on to state that industrial growth—which until then was viewed only as progress—was resulting in previously unsuspected and destructive pollution and an unsustainable depletion of nonrenewable natural resources.

The crisis has taken many forms. While in 1965 the prominent futurologists Kahn and Wiener,[8] speculating about the year 2000, made no mention of either pollution or environment,* at the time of revising this chapter a conference on ecology has just ended in Brazil that brought together representatives of over 140 countries and 76 heads of State, and a great number of nongovernmental organizations—an unprecedented event in the history of multilateral diplomacy.

Mostly, environmental problems are related to our exploitative and implicitly uncaring attitude in the face of nature and is manifest in such ways as the depletion of nonrenewable resources, the disappearance of thousands of plant and animal species and the deterioration of the atmosphere, lands and seas by pollution and erosion; thus, for instance, the ocean plankton, which may be said to constitute a large part of the earth lung (through its function of generating oxygen from carbon dioxide) is being poisoned; nuclear wastes threaten future generations, while the acid rain which begins to kill European trees reminds us of the uncertainty of our future subsistence as mammals who feed on plants. Impressive as an expression of human impotence in the face of the devastation of nature is the situation of rain forests. While attending a conference on the preservation of rain forests in Malaysia, some eight years ago, I remember the president of the University of Penang, who opened our meeting, remarking that during the time he had spoken thus far, approximately ten minutes, it could be esti-

---

The Year 2000: a framework for speculation on the next thirty-three years.

mated that fires (slash-and-burn) had devoured forests in Southeast Asia in an area comparable to that encompassed by the horizon. The situation is even more dramatic in the case of Brazil, the rain forests of which are unique in the world because of their more ancient origin and as a consequence have an unparalleled variety of species that are still only partly known. And then, there is the problem of ozone depletion and a possible global heating that will melt the polar ice caps, raise the level of the oceans and flood the world's great ports . . .

It is as if throughout our history we never had to worry about where to dump our garbage. There was always some place a little further from where we lived. Now that we have peopled the whole earth there is no place beyond, and we begin to choke in our own detritus.

The calamities increase in number. Naturally, the one of greatest concern is the security crisis. Just as there is no place where we can throw our garbage anymore, there are no distant lands to discover or alien peoples to conquer. The earth has been all discovered and conquered, and just as our polluting is turning against ourselves, also our conquering drive is turning back upon us. Wars and weapons, things which many considered (until a short time ago) an aspect of human nature, have now become lethal to a degree never before contemplated. It has been calculated that for every seventeen years of war in human history there has been one year of peace. But this incapacity for peace that has characterized our species has also become untenable because we now have a self-destructive capability which we have never had before. Knowing human beings and their imperfections, this incapacity now becomes more dangerous than ever. Sometime in the eighties I heard a U.S. general say that even if all the armaments on the face of the earth were eliminated, there would still remain sixty atomic submarines, each of which would have the capacity to destroy the major cities of the earth. It is also necessary to bear in mind the economic aspect of this situation: the cost of one of these submarines is equivalent to that of the combined budgets of twenty-three developing countries, and one intercontinental missile costs as much as it would cost to build thousands of schools in the underdeveloped world.

The list of problems could continue: there is world hunger, for example, related to overpopulation—which is, in turn, a factor behind pollution and competition for territory and resources. Overpopulation certainly needs to be considered one of the main problems of today and yet is in itself a consequence of a less recognized problem: our inability to control global affairs—a societal analog to what in the individual organism is a disturbance of organismic self-regulation—dependent on such factors as fragmentation, dehumanization and many others. And then, we should not let the new ecological and overpopulation problems and the urgent peace problem cause us to lose sight of the old and yet ever present problem of injustice in its many forms (what is usually labeled today as infringement of human rights) which continues to breed not only discontent, social unrest and wars but acts as a chronic traumatic situation on our species, crippling the quality of emotional life of individuals, generation after generation.

So there is a kind of madness in the present state of human affairs. People have become very concerned, especially in the last ten years. It is something which is discussed everywhere, and diverse diagnoses have been put forth. Many (Gabriel Marcel, Barbara Garson[9] among others) consider technocratic government the greatest of our ills. Theodore Roszak preferred to call it "technocratic totalitarianism." Willis Harman, in his book, *An Incomplete Guide to the Future*,[10] suggested that all of this has to do with the mentality of industrial man; he attempted to show that, beyond technology and the modern capitalistic economic machine, the way of life which we have created also entails a particular mentality and that this is itself responsible in the end for all those consequences which, despite many good intentions, seem difficult to resolve. More recently, Capra proposed, in his book *The Turning Point*,[11] that even more important than industrialism and the way of life that it entails is a one-sided *rationalism* and our mechanistic approach to the world and ourselves.

By the end of the last century Nietzsche had already pointed to the serious limitations of rationalism, and again in recent times there is much discussion on the subject, but in general Newton, Descartes and Aristotle end up being blamed, which seems to me unfair. Aristotle was an initiate in the mysteries; Descartes, in addition to having given us analytical geometry, was a profoundly intuitive and religious man and Newton was an alchemist. It is ironic that these highly intuitive individuals, who were less "linear" than most of us, end up being pointed out as the prime examples of the limitations of linear thinking. Yet it is very important that we recognize and question the fact that we attempt to manage our affairs and the world through the use of reason only.

Important as the issue of mind-change is, I doubt that in pointing to the over-rational mentality that has culminated in our technological age we have identified the ultimate root of the problem. I suspect, rather, the excessive rational bent of the diagnosis, which seems to imply a unidirectional interpretation of various emotional dispositions (such as greed and dominance) and of political ills (such as nationalism and the overdevelopment of bureaucracy) as complications of wrong thinking. True as it may be that cognition influences feeling and that worldviews (in the form of religion, philosophy and myth) have not only served to liberate and transform us but have also been used to rationalize and justify our pathologies, there is also truth in Marx's view of ways of thinking as "super-structure," and we can just as well think of rationalism as the outcome of greed: for anti-spiritual scientism and the tyranny of the linear mode may well be viewed as a sort of freezing of cognition in its utilitarian-analytic mode, and this, in turn, understood as a greedy fixation on survival to the detriment of the gratuitous and soul-nourishing activity of contemplation; we can certainly say that greed [or deficiency motivation or pre-genital (oral-anal)] libido exists in interdependence with the Cartesian vice of the technological era.

2 A Diagnosis

Yet I think that the search for a unified exploration of our cognitive, emotional and sociopolitical ills is valid.

We might say, simply (as I have throughout the years) that it is our *incapacity for human relationship* which supports our sick society and which has brought us to our crisis predicament. Anybody with a good grasp of dynamic psychology can conclude that it is our incapacity to love our neighbor, ourselves, and the highest values that militates against our sustaining truly brotherly relationships with those around us, and results in a sick society and a host of secondary problems. Yet we can still be more precise in our diagnosis if we address ourselves more exactly to what stands between us and our potential for brotherhood: the word "patriarchal" invites us to think that our failure to establish fraternal relationships lies in an obsolete *paternal/filial bond of authority/dependence supported by a tyranny of the paternal aspect over the maternal and the child-like* that renders us incapable of genuinely loving ourselves and others.

I have been exploring for a long time the view of "patriarchy" as the single root of industrial-mindedness, capitalism, exploitation, greed, alienation, our incapacity for peace and our destruction of the natural world. If we call our planetary condition a disease, I propose, then, as the diagnosis of our ills the patriarchal organization of the mind and of society.

To say that our problem is the "patriarchal order" is the same as saying that the problem is as old as civilization itself, which implies that we cannot expect freeing ourselves from our difficulties without questioning what we have been doing for a very long time. For only then can we aspire to change a structure so thoroughly and deeply entrenched that we tend to take our present way of being—the result of our conditioning—for our essential nature.

The theme of patriarchy was introduced over a century ago by Johann Jakob Bachofen (1815–1887),[12] Swiss philosopher of history and society whose work on Mother right and Primal Religion influenced anthropologists, the feminist movement, Nietzsche, Engels and others.

It is most remarkable that Bachofen was able to discover that a mother-centered world preceded the father-centered civilizations through the contemplation of scant piecemeal information such as old customs of various peoples reported by Herodotus and Thucydides. Through a combination of remarkable intuition and erudition he arrived at the formulation of a theory of social evolution in three stages. First, a "tellurian" stage of promiscuity and motherhood without marriage; then, in reaction to this, a "lunar" stage when marriage was instituted as a regulative principle and women took over the exclusive ownership of children and property—a stage coinciding with settled communities and the rise of agriculture; and finally a "solar" stage—the patriarchal—in which there is conjugal father right, a division of labor, individual ownership and the institution of the State.

Joseph Campbell says in his introduction to the English translation of *Myth, Religion and Mother Right* that to read mythology as Bachofen did, it was necessary "to cast aside one's contemporary, historically conditioned manner of thought and even of life." He quotes the mature Bachofen writing to his preceptor (through an autobiographic sketch written in response to his request): "that without a thorough transformation of our whole being, without a return to ancient simplicity and health of soul, one cannot gain even the merest intimation of the greatness of those ancient times and their thinking, of those days when the human race had not yet, as it has today, departed from its harmony with creation and the transcendent creator."

Master of archetypal psychology before the word was invented (which, by the way, he called *Grundgedanken*—fundamental thoughts), Bachofen had a deep influence on Joseph Campbell, who—with the etiquette of a college professor—was to give a severe blow to patriarchy through his ironic presentation of father-centered Middle Eastern fanaticism in the universal context of world religions and mythology. Because I do not doubt that Joseph Campbell was a decisive background to the inspiration of today's rising Goddess religion in the women's movement, I think that it is fair to see Bachofen as its cultural grandfather.

Bachofen's influence on anthropology was great, yet scarcely visible today in view of the fact that after lending the emerging science a powerful stimulus, his ideas came to be seen as somewhat passé.

After Morgan and others inspired by him inspired, in turn, a whole generation of anthropologists to address themselves to this question of cultural evolution, the question in time was felt to be insoluble. Anthropology became less interested in comparative studies, and more inclined to understand cultural characteristics in the meaning context of the specific society in which they occurred.

Anthropology (and perhaps most notably Malinowsky and Margaret Mead) has certainly made us acquainted with many living nonpatriarchal societies, but how much we can know of our prehistory through such old societies is not knowable. The most remarkable summation of what was known of mother-centered peoples by the time the topic lost interest to the specialists is contained in Robert Briffault's monumental work, *The Mothers*,[13] published in 1927. It was written to counter the then prevalent view that saw the patriarchal institution of the family as an expression of natural law—and this much he accomplished. To him we owe a shift in focus in anthropology from mother-rule or inheritance through the mother to the question as to whether the wife resides after marriage at the husband's house or vice-versa (patrilocy or matrilocy). It was he, too, that formulated the idea that marriage was originally a contract between groups, in which it was agreed that a man of one group might have sexual access to all the women of another group while being denied access to his own.

Though ethnologists have not found a living instance of "matriarchy" in the sense of female dominance comparable to what we know male dominance to be, it is still possible that women have had a more significant role during our prehistoric evolution.

More dramatic than the anthropological findings has been perhaps the confirmation of Bachofen's account through the archaeological findings from the Near East and old pre-Aryan Europe. This is particularly the case in connection with the agricultural revolution of the Neolithic and the preceding upper Paleolithic. Literally thousands of figures of women have been unearthed (sometimes called Venuses), fat pregnant women whose feet and arms are scarcely represented and who are almost nothing but a womb and in whom even the head seems little more than the apex of a triangle. Suggestive of icons, they are believed to allude to the procreative power of nature. The places in which they have been found over all of Europe suggest a generalized religious sentiment towards a feminine deity—a creative, procreative deity related to fertility that has been extensively investigated by Marija Giambutas.[14]

Also, in what is now Turkey, cities* dating from 6000 B.C. have been excavated in which, unlike later patriarchal cities, there are no signs to reveal that there were wars in them during a period of some fifteen centuries—when they were destroyed by the Indo-European migrations.

The stage of history that followed is now rather well known. The patriarchal Indo-European conquerors dominated the matristic** cultures through a supremacy afforded them through the mastery of two techniques: the domestication of the horse and iron metallurgy. It may be thought that these masculine cultures of the "iron age" correspond to a second stage of patriarchal organization, a further deteriorated stage in regard to the extent with which power was originally wielded—during the patriarchy of the bronze age as described in the *Iliad*.

Yet it is neither in the specialized domains of archaeology or ethnology that the word "patriarchy" has been most widely known. There can be no doubt that it is a word intimately connected to the women's movement. Though a name for the archenemy from the very beginning, at first it only seemed to stand for the enemy of *women*. Thus Eva Figes's *Patriarchal Attitudes*,[15] written in 1970, constitutes an indictment of male injustice and is an implicitly political book that compares male chauvinism to anti-Semitism and addresses itself to the benefit of the oppressed and the exploited.

In time, however, it seems to have come to be understood that the archenemy of women also deserves to be regarded an enemy of the children, and—since we all have been children— an enemy of all. Thus I find in Mary Daly's *Gyn/Ecology*[16] a reference to Françoise d'Eubonne's book *Le Féminisme ou la*

---

*Particularly the city of Catal Huyuk.

**I borrow Giambutas's word.

Mort[17] in which she coins the word "eco-féminism" and "maintains that the fate of the human species and of the planet is at stake, and that no male-led 'revolution' will counteract the horrors of overpopulation and destruction of natural resources." And she reflects forth in this essay on the "Meta-ethic of Radical Feminism": "I share this basic premise, but my approach and emphasis are different. Although I am concerned with all forms of pollution in phallotechnic society, this book is primarily concerned with the mind/spirit/body pollution inflicted through patriarchal myth and language on all levels. These levels range from styles of grammar to styles of glamour, from religious myth to dirty jokes, from theological hymns honoring the 'Real Presence' of Christ to commercial cooing of Coca-Cola as 'The Real Thing,' from dogmatic doctrines about the 'Divine Host' to doctored ingredient-labeling of Hostess cakes, from subliminal ads to 'sublime' art. Phallic myth and language generate, legitimate, and mask the material pollution that threatens to terminate all sentient life on this planet."

It is Mary Daly's contention that the eight basic sins in terms of which the fathers of the church spelled out the wrongness of the human mind exist in the context of *phallocracy* (as she calls the patriarchal aberration of society).

Riane Eisler—in *The Chalice and the Blade*[18]—has pointed even more explicitly to patriarchy as humankind's essential problem. Recapitulating the essential data from specialized research, Eisler reminds us that the patriarchal way, *far* from being natural to humankind, has constituted a fall from the "paradise" of our pre-patriarchal condition in Neolithic times. She offers us the notion that to speak of the patriarchal order is equivalent to speaking of a society that is based on domination, and such a world, founded on a predominance of the masculine—itself sanctioned by power—constitutes the central aberration of our culture. The importance of this sole idea makes *The Chalice and the Blade* a work of much greater weight than a mere popularization of anthropological and historical research would account for—perhaps important enough to justify the assertion by Ashley Montague that he has never recommended a book so much and that it "deserves to be considered the most important work since Darwin's *The Origins of the Species.*

Yet it is not from Eisler that I have taken my view of patriarchy as root of our macroproblem. My interest in the subject dates from the mid-fifties, and my inspiration was kindled by an older and little-known source: a fellow Chilean who was aware of the critical state of world affairs more than fifty years ago. Although I have chosen to give this chapter the simple title, "The Agony of the Patriarchal Order," I will be devoting the rest of it to Totila Albert and his vision of a tri-une society.

3 Totila Albert's Vision of a Tri-une Society

Totila Albert, born in Chile, became known as a sculptor in the years following World War I. Though he was called "the German Rodin" by his contemporaries in Berlin and may be regarded the best sculptor that Chile produced, different circumstances concurred against his becoming internationally known, and today most of his work (originally in plaster) has succumbed to the ravages of time.

At the age of 37 and upon the death of his father, Totila underwent a death-in-life that constituted a passage to a rebirth or—as he called it—"self-birth." After that he turned from sculpture to poetry, in the German language, and was lucky to be supported by friends in prewar Berlin while he devoted himself completely to the process of writing that now became the hub of his growing into a new life. Then he left Germany on the day before the declaration of World War II (and the closing of Germany's frontiers) and returned to Chile, the country of his birth.

Here he got married at 48, returned to sculpture for survival but also wrote poetry. A few people came to learn sculpture from him; mostly they came to treasure his healing nearness, but I am sure that by now he was more interested in shaking those he came in contact with and were willing to listen out of their "patriarchal slumber."

He was not a philosopher in the technical sense of the word, and arrived at his political intuition not through discursive thought, but as the end result of the long and dramatic process of inner development that had turned him, in the middle years of his life, from sculptor into poet and mystic. An early part of this process was a sort of inner alchemy, in which—after a mythic and yet very real "descent into hell" (that followed upon his father's death)—the internalized images of his father and mother came into dialogue with him and within him, and the relation between his "inner three" healed beyond the pattern of his childhood conditioning. Throughout his epic poem, *The birth of the I*, written in German (in Berlin) during the thirties, we can indirectly witness the process. An aspect of it was a moving from the parents of this world to "cosmic parents," to be born in the end—as a son of heaven and earth—into a new dimension of consciousness which he called *Die Musiche Raum* (the space of the Muses).

Later in life he would say that our biological parents are at the same time obstacles and potential vehicles to our connection with our universal ones. Since the death of his father had been like the lightning that sets a tree on fire—an inner death that was to bring him to a new life—he thought that the death of those whom we love most constitutes a pathway that life itself has placed before us for our spiritualization. I believe that historians of culture have reason enough to believe that this is so: death seems to stand as the beginning of all human religion.

During 1938, the shock of what happened around him in prewar Berlin brought Totila out of the "ivory tower" of his poetico-alchemical laboratory. In 1938 he wrote three "letters"—which, as I remember having heard him say—he would have wished some kindhearted patron would print and drop from the skies of Europe. Two of these letters are addressed to "mother" and "father" respectively, the third is from mother to son—but by now it is not to his personal parents that they are addressed, and "father" stands for the "absolute father"—the imperialistic "father principle." Better than defining the concept, I let the poetic language of the first of these letters convey it:

> Dear Mother
>
> My decision is already taken. Is it also yours? Everything I do is for your good. Do you also act in this manner in regard to me, your child? Or do you become implicated in actions that are damaging to me? I know that you are at my father's service. You do this out of the kindness of your heart. I know you want his good and mine. Yet this does not result in our well-being, for you support our provider, but it is from you that I receive the nourishment. Or is it not? So it was when I was in your womb. And not now? Has father taken over nourishment? He who produces it keeps it for himself?—Is it possible that he is not intending to feed me? Is he mainly wanting to make a business of my nourishment? He is not my nourisher then. Oh mother! What an ugly word I have just said! To make a business of our nourishment! That he cannot do. I don't want to believe it. But you do go shopping. You go to a store and pay money for my nourishment. Money! It is father who earns it. But how does he have time to earn money if he must plow, sow, harvest,

make bread? How does he have time to make money? Have you committed him earning it? And you have not retained for yourself the right to earn it? How is this so? Did you once lose this right? And you have conquered it again? Valiant mother, now that you earn money, how do you find time to carry me in your womb, nourish me and make my bed? What do I say? You must also wash me, dress me, teach me to walk. Walking. That I learned by myself. And I am too slow. I want to say you must also teach me to talk. Did you teach me first "Mama" or "Papa"? Or did I come to the world with these eternal sounds? When I close my mouth my lips are the one over the other and I do "M-m." Then I see your mild smile and I say "Ah." But the "M" is now sounded. You heard it and answered "Ma" and I said "Ma-ma," full of joy, and I discovered the mother tongue of all beings. But what was that about money? We did talk about money. How would I prefer to think about how I learned the hard and heavy syllable "Pa"? When I knew it, however, how did I like to repeat "Pa-pa" before your brilliant eyes? Let us talk about money on another occasion, dear mother. Your son.

Knowing about the imminent onset of war, Totila left for Chile with the last ship that left the coast of Germany, and once there, needed to return to his activity as a sculptor to earn his living.* In 1943, however, when we may think that Totila began to feel at home in the midst of his new circumstances and recovered from his deep grief, he continued to write out of the same intuition that had prompted his letters of 1938. He produced, in German, a series of 66 hymns bearing the title "Die Dreimal Unser" ("The Thrice Ours," or simply "The Three"),

---

*Moved by faith in the spiritual process and work that was emerging from Totila during his stay in Berlin, a circle of admiring friends had supported him from the time when he turned from sculpture to poetry ten years earlier.

items of political poetry—or mystico-political poetry, more precisely—which he conceived (as I remember hearing him say) as "verbal posters" destined to draw people's attention toward the dangerous obsolescence of the patriarchal order in which we are immersed.

"We no longer want governments and fatherlands"(1)—the first of these begins—"The earth presents us its shovels and weaves our garments"(2). Just as the first two lines (here condensed into one) involve a vision similar to that of Marx's ideal of a world without a state machinery supported in power and in which human needs may be satisfied, the last two verses remind us of Jesus's preaching on the lilies of the field and the birds that have no need to worry about their sustenance: they entail an optimist view to the effect that just as nature fulfills its functions without charging a payment, human beings integrated into the natural order (and attuned to their deepest nature) constitute generous and loving prolongations of nature itself, so that "nobody would deprive himself of the pleasure of being useful." "We don't want a prison anymore"(3), he continues to say in reference to the implicit condition of slavery of the individual under the patriarchal order in society and in the mind. "Neither customhouses nor slaughterhouses, Father"(4).* To speak of customhouses is to speak of borders: not only doing business with the goods of life, but division of the world into "fatherlands" constitute, for Totila, a fundamental aspect of our problem. "Slaughterhouse," naturally, makes reference to the fact that wars are obligatory, i.e., override any

---

*(1) Wir wollen keine Staaten mehr!
   Wir wollen keine Vaterlander!
(2) Die Erde reicht den Spaten her
   Und webt uns allen die Gewander.
(3) Wir wollen kein Gefanguis mehr
(4) Kein Zuchthaus und kein Schlachthaus, Vater

individual objections to them, regardless of whether the "absolute father" whom we collectively serve manifests in the form of the old-fashioned tyrant, or modern and supposedly democratic government. In the last two lines of this stanza, Totila addresses this father, demanding his return as "pure divine counselor"(5) that he originally was before the patriarchal disorder.*

Totila's view differed from that of political anarchists in that the world that he conceived, even though without government, required administration. He shared with the more lucid anarchists, however, a faith that individual freedom blossoms in a loving expression and is compatible with the common good: "Freedom is the straight path along which the binding duties tread"(6), he says. And still further along, in the fifth stanza of this first hymn, he exclaims, "Away with money, away with the business of slaving women and slaving children! You want to deprive forever the dreaming sleeper of his awakening."(7)**

Just as the ant has no awareness of its limited freedom, neither does roboticized humankind have an awareness of enslavement; but for one who awakens to the true condition of society and human relations, this condition of enslavement of the inner child and of the feminine aspects of the psyche to the dictates of an imposed authority becomes very obvious. Yet it is no longer the authority of the *pater familias*, the Pope, or the emperor that bears down on ordinary people (a condition to

---

*(5) Wir forden deine Wiederkehr
   Als reinen himmlischen Berater

**(6) Die Freiheit is die rechte Bahn
   Auf der die strengen Pfichten laufen
 (7) Fort mit dem Geld! Fort das Geschaft
   Mit Sklavenmuttern, Sklavenkindern!

The Agony of the Patriarchal Order

which Totila used to refer as the "degenerate patriarchate"). He ends this first hymn—which I have chosen to scan, for it is emblematic of the whole work—with, "Such, however, is the meaning of the dream: to realize the dream upon awakening! Conquered already is the earth, let us turn it into a home!"(8)*

Upon returning to Chile from the country where he had been sent by his parents at the age of eleven, Totila continued to write in German; then, he produced a volume of poetry in Spanish, but it was clear that his mastery of the language was not comparable to his mastery of German. The outcome of his frustration, we may surmise, was the writing of some pages in prose that he entitled "Prologue," and this may be considered a prologue to the hymns as much as to the political poems in Spanish, yet constitutes, rather, a manifesto. I quote from its opening:

> In the search for the cause of the lack of unity among human beings and of the great confusion that is part of the conditions of humankind, state and church have been criticized but never has the last step been taken: placing the responsibility upon the creator of these institutions who through the use of power has given himself absolute value and claimed the right to the life and death of the family, which he has considered his property and of whose goods he has taken possession. It is now time that we don't concern ourselves only with the symptoms but with the sickness itself, and that we acknowledge in the patriarchal order the origin of our human imperfections and the artificiality of our form of life.

---

*(8) Das aber ist Sinn im Traum:
　Den Traum erfullen beim Erwachen!
　Erobert ist der Erdenraum
　Zur Heimat wollen wir ihn machen!

As I have already said, Totila's thinking was not that of a professional philosopher, but that of a visionary. I could, with different words, say that his political view was a corollary of a spiritual experience. The "message of the three" (as he used to call his social vision), was the corollary of the perception of something that practically every spiritual tradition has known and considered a mystery. Let us call it the "mystery of trinity"—though in a wider sense than that suggested by an all-too-dogmatic understanding of the Christian trinity.

Trinity is one of the great truths concerning the universe and man that has been recognized in practically every culture, and is only a "mystery" in that it cannot be arrived at through discursive thinking alone but through an experience in practice accessible to a few (for it entails a long previous odyssey).

Different traditions formulate trinity in different ways. We are all familiar with the Christian trinity, and may be familiar with the Trimurti of the Hindus: the vision of deity as creator, preserver and destroyer. Another version of trinity, originating in India as well, stems from the Samkya philosophy, which speaks to us of three *gunas* or strands that are interwoven in everything that exists in the process of becoming—one active, the other passive and the third balancing. Still another vision, that of Taoism, shows us man as the son of "heaven" and "earth"—cosmic principles that are also termed *yang* and *yin* and discussed as light and dark, creative and receptive, masculine and feminine.

When Totila Albert spoke of three "principles," he preferred to call them father, mother, and child. For this, to him, was the language that best corresponded to the natural fact that in life "as above, so below"—i.e., the fact that the most intangible truths are echoed in a visible crystallization. Not only did he have in mind the embodiment of the universal principles of father, mother, and child in the biological and social beings that we designate through these words, but, most particularly, in the structure of the human body.

> Already in the fecundated egg are to be found the three components in potential form.
>
> In the outer embryonic layer, the ectoderm, which originates the skin, the sense organs, and the central nervous system and that provides us with the connection with the macrocosm, we can recognize the father principle.
>
> In the inner embryonic layer, the endoderm, of which are formed the viscera, and which constitutes the connection to the earth, is manifested the mother principle.
>
> In the middle embryonic layer, the mesoderm, formed in its turn of one sheath turning towards the ectoderm and another facing the endoderm, and from which derive the future self-support (skeleton), the system of action (muscular system), the life of impulse and circulation (heart), and responsibility in the preservation of the species (gonads), we find the embodiment of the child principle.
>
> With these principles is the human being born and can only develop harmoniously when after being born these three components are fostered in the same measure.

There was also in his conception a vision of history: a vision according to which, just as we now live in a patriarchal age, we have gone through a matriarchal period, and even before that (something I have not heard cultural scholars formulate, yet is consistent with the information that we have) an original "filiarchal" age.

> In the whole history of humanity, however, the balance of these three components has been disturbed.

In the first period, through the emphasis on the filial component (filiarchal age: nomads who move in search of spring and sacrifice their ageing parents along the way who no longer have the skills and ability to continue along with them—the time that the mythology of all peoples knows as an age of gold and eternal youth).

In the second period, through an emphasis on the mother component (matriarchal age: projection of the microcosmic home—the womb—to the macrocosm; sedentary life, agriculture and architecture come, the beginnings of "culture"; exclusion of the father from the home and the reaction to it, the formation of masculine leagues outside of the home, initiation of masculine youths to these groupings, invention of instruments for hunting and fishing, weapons, and the beginning of investigation of natural forces and of their control).

In the third period, through an emphasis on the father component (patriarchal age: discovery and appropriation of the earth, conquest of the maternal home, fall of the matriarchal order—referred to in mythology as "the struggle of light against darkness. Institution of the absolute power of the father).

In contrast to traditional myth of *earthly paradise,* Totila's notion envisions human wholeness as a potential condition not yet realized. His vision of a necessary balance between three inner principles implicitly answers not only the lack of healthy partnership between the sexes but also the authoritarianism between the generations that has characterized patriarchal society no less than male dominance. Beyond the valid sociopolitical issues of authoritarianism, however, I think it has the merit of emphasizing the intra-psychic dimension: it is the *inner* balance between "Father," "Mother" and "Child" that he regarded as the sign of the maturity of our species and the necessary support for a tri-une society.

I am inclined to think that the view of a deterioration of society after a pre-patriarchal, equalitarian paradise entails an idealization of matristic prehistory comparable to the idealization of the patriarchal order that was offered to us, also fairly recently, by Ken Wilber in *Up from Eden*.[19] The best support available to us as a basis for imagining what may have been the Neolithic world is offered to us by today's agrarian matrilineal societies. The observation of these does not make us feel that we stand before a flowering of human nature; they rather make us recall Erich Fromm's interpretation of this stage of humankind as an "incestuous union with the earth" that fosters stagnation.

True as it may be that "matriarchy" is a misnomer, for domination is a predominantly masculine trait and historically a masculine invention, when Totila adopts Bachofen's word "matriarchy" his meaning has shifted to that of a social state of affairs resulting from the *inner* dominance of the mother principle. It is not through individual domination that power has expressed itself in mother-centered communities, but through group tyranny—a mentality in which the individual is entirely devoured through its bond with the community. There are those who think of the Neolithic with nostalgia, as an ideal of perfect democracy (and why not use the Neolithic for such a beautiful dream?) yet anthropologists almost unanimously tell us that this is not consistent with what we know about the mother-centered world of the planters—in which the individual is entirely subordinated to the group and its interpretation of the needs of nature. The institution of human sacrifice, which may be taken as visible embodiment of this surrender to the community—and supposedly to the balance of nature (in the name of the divine)—stands before us as a giveaway of the imbalance at this stage of human evolution. Only if we think of the mother-centered period as non-optimal can we understand that those who carried forward the patriarchal revolution may have symbolized it as a victory of light over darkness, as in the heroic adventure of Perseus who severs the Gorgon's paralyzing head.

A lucid social philosophy must acknowledge the evolutionary aspect of the transition from the matriarchal to the patriarchal order, along with an acknowledgement of a counter-evolutionary aspect—a fallenness, an exuberant pathology, a deterioration. Joseph Campbell proposed that we understand this pathology as a "mythical inflation,"[20] an expression which he introduced in his discussion of the Egyptian divine kings who brought family and servants along into their tombs (a remote antecedent to the more recent practice of suttee). We know from records of spiritual life that pathological grandiosity arises as a complication to spiritual experience at a certain level of unripeness, and in the same way we may imagine that a momentous breakthrough in consciousness went along with the perpetration of crimes in its name. Thus Wilber has some reason in celebrating the victory of Zeus over the serpent Typhon—the independence of human spirit in the face of nature—*transcendence* in the face of mother Nature, a cosmic indifference in the face of Eros, a supreme Apollonian detachment after the fullness of Dionysian surrender.

The sky Gods were born—Dyaus Pitar, Jupiter, Indra, Jehova. Can we doubt that the first form of the patriarchal order (an echo of which would be the classical civilizations) was the expression of an evolutionary thrust in the human mind? But let us look at the price of that pearl, and the strife about it.

Wilber's* criticism of the "solar" patriarchal regime is mostly that of human sacrifice, but we know sacrifice to have

---

*Echoing Gebser's evolutionary perspective.

been a legacy of a mother-centered prehistory. He does not tell us anything of military sacrifices, and the chronic sacrifice implied in poverty—still another manifestation of the dominion of the strong over the weak. This dominion began (as Gerda Lerner has pointed out) with the enslavement of women, continued with generalized slavery, and then with later forms of social inequality such as Marx indicated intrinsic to our malaise. It seems to me that Wilber oversimplifies, both in his view of collective transformation and in his view of individual transformation—when he wants to conceive of both as a linear progression, a simple ladder up to heaven.

The classical interpretation of history before Darwin was that of a continuous falling. In esoteric circles, and in the traditions that have come to us through Ovid, for instance, or through the book of Daniel or in the Indian doctrine of the *yugas*, there is the notion of a fall from "a golden age" to an age of silver, in which feminine values became emphasized; then, a bronze age is mentioned as a stage preceding our "iron age" or "kaliyuga." The Hindus conceive of the iron age or the "age of the she-wolf" as one in which we bounce up after hitting bottom—one in which (just as in St. John's Book of Revelation) we must go through the worst before giving birth to a New Age.

Such was the view of universal decadence until the time when the vision of an evolution of the species lead Spencer and others to conceive of an evolution of society. The euphoria of discoveries and scientific progress, the accelerated growth of knowledge and the conquest of nature certainly contributed to make the idea of progress strongly felt. It is in this manner that Bachofen and later Gebser (echoed today by Wilber) speak to us more of an ascent than a descent. Yet I think that it is more appropriate to understand the unfoldment of history through the simile of a plant that has contracted a viral infection upon sprouting from its seed: not only does a process of growth take place, but there is at the same time a "parasitic" or "cancerous" growth: the growth of its disease.

In Totila's view (which echoes Bachofen's view of three stages) the fall into the patriarchal order has only been the last of three successive falls in the course of our history. The mother-centered state of affairs had not involved the establishment of an ideal condition, however idyllic the mother-centered world may seem to us in our time of patriarchal tyrannies and wars, and there also had been, to him, a fall *into* the mother-centered world. And even, before this, it was appropriate to speak of a fall or pathology at the time of the arising of an early youth-centered society in which there is a dominance of the over-individualistic child-principle which involves a dominance of aggression over love and of action over feeling and intellect. We know of such a condition in recent times from the example of Eskimos, who used to abandon their parents in the polar ices in order to continue along their annual migration.

Rather than inviting us to attempt the recovery of a past partnership between the sexes, Totila proposes (adopting the happy expression of Salvador Paniker[21]) a "retroprogressive" solution. Retrogressive, in that it aspires to a reintegration of conditions and values from pre-patriarchal times; progressive, in that—as Totila used to say—the harmony between our three components is not something that we have had a chance to live yet—neither during the matriarchal age nor during the savage stage of animalistic individualism that we entered when our ancestors adopted a view of the world compatible with the rude battle for survival in the ice ages. Far from recommending a return to a mother-centered condition or even the condition of a lost paradise, thus, Totila would summon us to try something radically new, the creation of a society such as we have not known throughout our history of successive imbalances, each of which has a been a functional reaction in face of the traumatic conditions of the planet.

Like the old prophets, and also like Marx, Totila Albert believed at least in the possiblity of a healing and flowering of our species. Even more significantly, he offered us a vision of that which the Judeo-Christian tradition has called "the Kingdom of God," a vision in which the earth belongs to the three that we are, and in which it is essentially three who love each other on earth, illuminated through the cognition of divine trinity.

While patriarchal society is a hierarchic condition characterized by the institution of the State—that is to say, the control of the individual and the group (in the best cases) by a gifted and expert few—and while the matriarchal world has characterized itself by the control of the individual by the many (the clan), we can speak of a child-centered, filiarchal condition in which there is a predominance of the control of the individual by himself, with neglect of group bonds and without charismatic authority over-control. Alternatively, we may conceive the ideal world as one in which there exists a heterarchical relationship between the three components at the individual, familial, and cultural level. In the political realm, we may conceive of this as involving a balance between the solutions of exclusive obedience to self, to community, to central government; this amounts to a balance between the forms of government which in extreme form we know as anarchy, dictatorship of the proletariat (or of public opinion, or the market) and tyranny.

4 Toward a Tri-une Society

If it is true, as I have been claiming, that we would do well in moving towards a harmonization of father, mother, and child (within ourselves and in our social world) then we have grounds to feel optimistic, for it may be said that the revolution of the child against the father started a long time ago, and the reintegration of the feminine principle has perhaps been the most significant characteristic of the modern cultural revolution.

Indeed, not only feminism, but a generalized expression of love of the earth and an ecological awareness, the emergence of groups, the tendency towards a more participatory democracy, and an increasing interest in emotional healing, together with the rediscovery of the body and its value, may be interpreted as a return of the mother principle.

Modern thinkers from theology (Matthew Fox) to feminism (Barbara Mor[22]) have already put forward such an interpretation of our more recent revolution. Specifically speaking of the ecological issue (and proposing it as a paradigm of our modern, retroprogressive orientation toward the origin), Salvador Paniker[23] observes that here, too, we see the resurgence of the mother and the Neolithic spirit. He says in one of his essays:

> Well then, it could be said that the ecological revolution tends to return things to their proper place. It might be said that the ecological revolution puts an end to a certain phallic aggression, and implies even a certain recovery of the "religiosity of the mother" (that stands in contrast to the classical monotheisms of Judaism and Islam).

Similarly, we may say that the desirable liberation of the child principle has been taking place for centuries. It is not exactly the case that the revolutions we have gone through since the Renaissance "have only put the child in the place of the father," as Totila used to say. It is also true that since the advent of Renaissance humanism an unquestionable liberation has been taking place, major stages of which have been protestantism, the abolishment of divine kingship, romanticism, movements of national independence and civil rights, student and youth movements (sexual freedom included), etc. What has been taking place is, unquestionably, a gradual crumbling down of authoritarianism. The counterculture and the human potential movement, we may say, have been one of the most significant stages in this liberation movement, for what was the seeker's counterculture of California in the sixties is permeating the Western world more and more.

I remember having heard Totila call himself more than once an optimist, in spite of his deep sorrow in the face of daily news and his wish to shake his contemporaries out of complacency. His optimism was not compatible with his realism vis-à-vis the critical human predicament and consisted in a faith that we have the resources and the potential to let go of our "patriarchal vessel" before it sinks.

He would have liked the analysis which was made known by the efforts of Buckminster Fuller, to whom it seemed important that we know that the natural resources at our disposal are enough to provide our whole world population with housing, food and energy, provided that we use the available technology wisely. It seems hopeful to know that with only putting an end to our misallocation of resources and knowing how to overcome the inertia of the system, we may be able to solve our material problem. I suspect that it is also important to know this because our vision of scarcity, a view to the effect that the goods of the earth will not suffice for all, has contributed to the exaltation of egocentrism, thus creating an artificial scarcity that feeds the vicious circle.

Not only the Jewish and Christian worlds have been messianic; the Hindus believe in the coming of a golden age, the ancient Mexicans prophesied the return of Quetzalcoatl, and Buddhism expects the appearance of a future Buddha of love. I personally do not look upon this as an irrational idea or only as a pacifier in the face of pain and death. We may view it as an intuition of our potential. The thought that we may come to unfold and actualize our true potential recommends itself to our mind like many scientific truths: it is aesthetically appealing and simple.

Yet we should not let the enthusiasm of an optimistic anticipation lead us to a complacent passivity. We must not (as a Spanish saying goes) "fall asleep on our laurels," congratulating ourselves that we are in an Aquarian Age in which everything will take care of itself; nor should we think that we have already undergone the great social transformation or that we are even at the brink of it, and that everything will work itself out in time.

The way out that Totila envisioned for the patriarchal order was not that of an Oedipal turning against the absolute father, but rather a refusal to obey him. Yet he knew well that for a "civil disobedience" in the face of technocracy to be possible, there is necessary the support of an inner change and liberation.

Being able to obey heaven through one's own heart is something that can only be achieved by the individual, through a psychological and spiritual process that can take a long time. Totila certainly did not believe that the external change that we need could happen without such inner transformation. He wanted so much to stress this, that in his prologue he says, "the Father, Mother and Child principles are independent of gender and age."

He spells them out in terms of functions. The function of the paternal principle is that of "fecundating, producing, giving shape to the gift of life from bread to art"; maternal functions are those of "receiving, nourishing, educating, and surrendering the complete being to life"; while the filial functions are those of "developing, learning, desiring, and being free."

All too commonly, I think, the early story of the women's movement was one of competition for male prerogatives in which there continued to operate that implicit "mismeasure of women" (to borrow Carol Tavris's expression[24]), according to which patriarchal standards continued to be unquestioned, and functions or qualities linked to femininity undervalued. The very fact of sexual differences became taboo to an egalitarianism that seemed to require sameness. Today we know that male and female nervous systems can be as different as male and female bodies, that already at birth women are (statistically speaking) more relational and less aggressive, and in the adult male there is more specialization of the cerebral hemispheres, while in the woman a more developed *corpus callosum* allows for greater interhemispheric coordination. Precisely because there is such a relationship it is important that women are not excluded from the decision-making process in affairs that concern us all. We only need to correct the chauvinistic interpretation of these differences as a male superiority. Fortunately the new feminism embraces an appreciation of differences and orients itself to the understanding of complementarity and the improvement of communication between the sexes (as in Deborah Tannen's engaging book, *You Just Don't Understand*[25]). Yet we should beware of absolutizing differences. Totila's statement to the effect that Father, Mother, Child are independent of gender or age reminds us that, related as they may be in general, they are not necessarily linked at the individual level— and each one of us should be appreciated for his or her specific bundle of dispositions. And mostly our task should consist not only in our leveling of the balance of power between the sexes, but in the humanization of the inner components.

What can we do, then, to speed up our transition from the hierarchical, patriarchal organization of our mind, towards a heterarchical, three-centered organization of father-mother-child?

5 What Can We Do?

I think that it is desirable that we all ponder the corollaries of a tri-une vision (inner and outer) of the Kingdom, and that those in the political domain would be most specially advised to give the vision a chance, for in view of the critical situation that we are undergoing, it behooves each of us to ask himself or herself what one may do and it is likely that our collective creativity will make a difference.

As I share some thoughts in this regard, I will not tarry on such things as have been often repeated, such as the evils of technology, patriarchal nationalism, the cost of the disunion of overpatriotic sovereign nations.

Certainly nationalism and patriotism are something comparable to the aberration of egocentric individualism raised to the collective sphere, an attitude appropriately defined by Erich Fromm as one of "putting one's own nation above humanity, above principles of truth and justice" and something very different from a loving appreciation of one's own nation. "Love towards one's own country that is not part of love of humanity," Fromm asserted, "is not love, but an idolatrous cult." We certainly need a planet that is politically and economically unified, and it is not necessary to be a Marxist to acknowledge the obsolescence of the sovereign state. Certainly, too, we are well on the way towards a balance between the sexes and between the generations, and it is to be expected that we may reach a world without the profit motive—one in which the motivation behind action is instinctive and loving and not contaminated through insecurity, neurotic greed, anxiety over survival, and false values.

It is not on such things that I want to focus principally, however, for it has become clear enough that even the most inspired revolution fails if it is not supported by a change within the human being, and that the society towards which we aspire can only be constituted by transformed individuals.

To begin with the more obvious: if it is "the harmonization of the three" within ourselves that is to constitute the gateway towards social change, it would be desirable that the process of such individual transformation be collectively sponsored.

Fortunately, the transformation process that is possible for a human being is one that has been known by at least a few throughout our history, and is being better and better understood and elucidated. I think that also, at the individual level, the view of this process as the death of the patriarchal ego and the emergence of the balanced trinity, of which Totila Albert speaks to us, may be inspiring.

Though the therapeutic and spiritual endeavors hardly require propaganda at this time, a time which has been characterized as one of questioning, it would be very desirable for the process of transformation to be generally understood as our most vital need, worthy of being deeply investigated and nurtured. Naturally, a wise government, whose wisdom did not only consist in knowing what to do, but in being able to do (that is to say, knowing how to counteract the inertia of the system), would be one that puts into practice the recognition of the political value of individual transformation.

How could it support it? How can this process of individual evolution, that is becoming so vital for the quantum leap beyond our crisis, be supported?

The human potential movement has been criticized for being accessible only to the elite (or, at least, the well-favored), and this is true of the therapeutic in general—inasmuch as public health has limited itself and concentrated principally on the physical aspects of medicine and when it comes to psychotherapy it has focused on symptoms and adjustments rather than growth and not taken advantage of the more modern resources. It is possible then to glimpse a future public health that strongly supports itself in consciousness-raising groups—not political but psychological groups, comparable to those that have arisen in the realms of feminism or in relation to the cure of addictions—yet designed and oriented to the specific task of contributing to the public psychological health of the poor.

Psychology has been bringing in successive contributions that are very pertinent to the subject of our inner fragmentation, and it may be said that it has also become more efficient in its contributions to the process of personal reintegration. Already the Freudian view of a psychological split between a superego "introjected" from the culture and a biological "id" addresses itself to the same issue as Totila when he points to the tyranny of the father principle over the mother principle. Transactional Analysis, inspired by the Freudian school, already approximates the language he proposed, contemplating the old Freudian triad in the alternative terms of parent, child and adult.

We could generally say that the organization of the mind indicated by post-Freudian psychologies are alternative descriptions of the patriarchal organization of the mind, one in which a healthy love toward oneself has turned into basic self-rejection from an inner tyrant ("top-dog" in the language of Fritz Perls) with regard to our impulses, and more generally, an inner rejection between intra-psychic fragments. In the Gestalt view implicitly cited already, the fundamental issue of the work is precisely the integrative encounter between "top-dog" and "under-dog"—the oppressor and the oppressed—to reach a condition that Perls called "organismic self-regulation."

Just as the body knows how to breathe without our having to tell ourselves, "now breathe in, now breathe out," also in the world of personal relations there are many things we could, so to say, leave in the hands of nature. This is an idea even Rogers took beyond the internal politics of the psyche, thinking it valid for human groups as well; that if there is enough time, even groups self-regulate. The patriarchal organization of the mind (described by Freud as our universal predicament) is then one in which we exist in a police state in which a superego tells us, "I accept you and love you if you do things in such and such a way." This is a state of affairs in which our superego (which is "us," after all) considers us potentially evil and guilty and not worthy of the trust of being allowed our freedom. This state of the mind exists in interaction with moralism, so that as Lao Tse most eloquently put it (when he spoke of the Tao's virtue of deep spontaneity), "When the original harmony was lost, laws arose."

A corollary to the proposition that the key to our liberation—as much psychospiritual as sociocultural and political—may lie in our ability to integrate the father, mother, and child components in ourselves, is the idea that it is critical for us to develop a synthesizing agent, a reconciling among our intrapsychic and biosocial components. If we are to move from a hierarchical order to a heterarchical, three-centered order (as Gurdjieff hoped some decades ago with his creation of the Institute for the Harmonious Development of Man), if in other words—as Totila Albert used to say—we need a world in which father, mother, and child within us and in the human family love one another, it would seem that the essential element is love itself, that capacity to say "yes" in the face of the other, and also, as Buber has underlined, an ability to say "you," acknowledging the other as subject. If there is to be integration, it is necessary that father, mother, and child, in the different levels, not only communicate among each other, but as in the figures composing the Taoist yin-yang (one white with a black dot, the other black with a white dot), each may bow before the other, and even recognize the other as the deepest in itself.

Totila Albert's vision is also inspiring when it suggests the importance of speaking of *loves*, in plural, of qualities or primordial forms of love. Father-love is oriented "heavenwards," to the world of principles, ideas, and ideals. Mother-love is oriented to nature, to individuality, and loves not according to merits but according to needs. Child-love, on the other hand—so pathologized in our world, inasmuch as the love bond with the parents is interrupted and replaced with a bond of resentment and idealized dependency—is characterized by grateful receptivity and awe.

Refining this thought further, we may say that an intrapsychic love between the father, mother, and child principles is necessary so that there may be also a harmony in the human family and one among the paternal, maternal, and filial values. Totila expressed this in a bas-relief titled *The Bird of Returning* that existed on the facade of a public building in Santiago until it was destroyed toward the end of the military dictatorship in the eighties. In it, the paternal and maternal were assimilated to two wings that, through their polarity, permit the individual to move forward in flight.

More concretely, over the wings of a condor that carries the forward pointing Son lies on the left the mother pointing down (to earth and to the son), and on the right the father, pointing to heaven. Let us say that, if our usual condition is that of an infantile fixated state in which we regressively maintain a relation of need and ambivalence toward our childhood parents,* the healthy child that potentially lies within us can, through its love toward the inner father and inner mother, make the qualities of father-love and mother-love its own, and thus integrate the love of heaven and the love of earth, the love of wisdom and the love of nature, the love of divine transcendence, and the love of divine immanence.

---

*The mature condition is one of liberation from the impact of all our childhood conditionings.

The Bird of Returning, Totila Albert

Though Christianity is "a religion of love" that has inspired many throughout history and propelled some into sainthood, it is necessary to recognize that just as it has come to us after its time of greatest patriarchal and inquisitorial distortion (when the church severed the gnostic and esoteric roots of our civilization) it has been of little yield in terms of salvation capacity. Historical Christianity, it must be admitted, has failed in respect to the creation of a world ruled by love.

In his prologue to *Androcles and the Lion*[26] (subtitled "Why Not Give Christianity a Try"), Bernard Shaw said that Christ's proposition of considering love as the fundamental norm might seem very reasonable to us after twenty centuries during which this presumed Christianity has carried out its politics in the style of Barabbas. He writes the following:

> The question seems a hopeless one after two thousand years of resolute adherence to the old cry of "Not this man, but Barabbas." Yet it is beginning to look as if Barabbas was a failure, in spite of his strong right hand, his victories, his empires, his millions of money, and his moralities and churches and political institutions . . . But he has had one quaint triumph. Barabbas has stolen his name and taken his cross as standard. There is a sort of compliment in that. There is even a sort of loyalty in it, like that of the brigand who breaks every law and yet claims to be a patriotic subject of the king who makes them.

And he adds later:

> I am not more of a Christian than Pilate was and that you are, dear reader" (Bernard Shaw declared himself an atheist) "and yet, just as Pilate, I much prefer Jesus to Annas and Caiphas. I am ready to admit that after contemplating the world and human nature for about 60 years, I don't see any way out of the misery of the world aside from that

which Christ's will would have found if he had tackled the task of a modern statesman.

Totila Albert was critical before every form of organized religion. But even if institutional churches, yielding to the patriarchal spirit of various cultures, have remained impotent in the face of war and other evils, I think that we must not deny the inseparability of the *spiritual* with regard to the therapeutic and the process of human unfoldment in general. The problem is that however true it may be that love is the solution to our problems, it may be said of it what is also said of the gold of alchemists: to make it, it is necessary to have it. In view of this situation it seems that we may profit very much from an age-old discovery of oriental traditions that now transpersonal psychology is making its own: that for love to emerge we need to learn to "stop the machinery" of our ego, and, more generally speaking, pacify "our passions" through the practice of detachment and, more precisely, through the arts of meditation.

We can define meditation in many ways, according to our preference for emphasizing one or another of its components, but to the extent that it may be legitimate to establish a contrast between devotion and meditation, let us say that just as devotion entails the cultivation of love, of surrender, and a sacralizing attitude, meditation entails the cultivation of mental quiet, awareness, and nonattachment. If it is true that we may speak of love as a synthesizing or integrative principle (just as Plato in his *Symposium* spoke of Eros), we can recognize the reconciling principle under a completely different guise. Just as in the human embryo, the mesoderm is constituted from a sheath turned towards the ectoderm and another turned towards the endoderm, likewise that in the psychological realm the reconciling principle also has two faces: one is its "maternal face," and the other, "paternal." Thus we may say that love is part of a bipolar phenomenon. Tibetan Buddhism has acknowledged as much by making the balance between wisdom and compassion (or in other words, between love and that detachment that arises before the "understanding of nothingness") a central statement of its spiritual pedagogy.

Love, then, exists in the context of a polarity of love and nonattachment, which superficially appears to us as a contradiction, yet more deeply considered, constitutes a complementarity. True love can only emanate from self-surrender and self-giving. Also the converse is true. There is no better way to reach detachment than through love. To speak of a polarity of love and nonattachment is to speak of that polarity that in mythology appears to us sometimes as a coupling of love and death, or a metaphysical marriage between death and life itself.

Just as Christianity is among all religions a religion of love, Buddhism is a religion of nonattachment par excellence, and offers us instruction along a deep and little-known path that consists not in doing this or that, but rather in developing a capacity to not do. In a certain way while meditating, one stops doing this or that, and if one becomes skilled enough to pacify one's mind and truly not do anything, one already has a panacea: he or she can then do anything. Of course, it is not so easy, but possible, and proven through centuries of spiritual discipline among Indian, Taoist and Buddhist yogis.

Northrop[27] tells us that one of the most important historical events in our time is the unification of values of East and West and the integration of the Northern and Southern hemispheres. It is in light of the first that I think we must view the coming of Buddhism to the West. It seems to me that just as some Christian spiritual directors have recognized the value of Buddhist meditation as a complement to the traditional spiritual practices, and just as psychotherapists have recognized the great value of the Buddhist way as a complement to interpersonal psychotherapy, this spiritual nontheistic approach may, through its resonance with our present-day scientific language, constitute not only an invaluable inspiration but a bridge between our own Judeo-Christian/Greco-Roman heritages.

If I'm not mistaken in giving such importance to this phenomenon of assimilation of the Buddhist vision by the Western culture (mostly now at the level of specialists and pioneers in the inner quest), it seems that we must also realize the great importance of a more recent phenomenon: the exodus of Tibetans from their land as a consequence of the Chinese invasion in 1958. For it seems to me that among the peoples of the earth, the ones who have specialized further than any other in the cultivation of consciousness have been the Tibetans—who a long time ago closed their borders to the world to turn their land into a sort of advanced spiritual hothouse, until the Chinese communist invasion brought with it genocide and the destruction of the temples. Many Tibetans then ended their isolation and spread out to India and then to other countries of the world as the seeds of certain plants spread upon the bursting of the mature fruits. It seems to me that the present Tibetan diaspora constitutes a potential gift of great value to those who know how to profit from it, and the enlightened leaders of the world should do well in being mindful of the situation.*

But to promote spirituality is not the same thing as—and goes beyond—supporting the churches of the world. More important is a clear acknowledgement that religiosity in the deeper sense of the word is an indispensable nourishment in a sane society; however true it may be that our religion has constituted an "opiate of the people," as Marx stated, as a result

---

*Let it be said, by the way, that the commercial alliances with China have mattered more to most nations to date so that only India, Mexico, and Nepal recognize the Dalai Lama as the political chief of Tibet.

of its message of "giving to Caesar what is Caesar's due" (by the way, Totila never believed that Jesus truly said such a thing), it is also a truth that religious people assert in saying that "man does not live by bread alone."

Both our technocrats and our Marxists need to keep it especially in mind—for Totila's statement concerning Marxism—a "religion of the stomach" may well be applied to both; thus with a Left and a Right that are equally stomach-centered, it behooves us to know how to differentiate between religion and spirituality, and know how to appreciate what is valid and constructive in all the traditions of the past that are now converging in our emergent culture.

With regard to this, Willis Harman's analysis in his recent book, *Global Mind Change*,[28] seems to me quite timely, when in considering growing unemployment he asserts that we cannot hope for other than its further increase, but that this should not concern us as it is conceivable that in the age of information and robotization we are entering, a large part of our subsistence work can be accomplished for us. And inasmuch as increasing unemployment can only lead to malaise for those who do not know how to make use of it, he also suggests that the possibility of leisure in the future constitutes a valuable opportunity, an invitation to return to a view of life which has as its primordial focus the realization of the highest values and the development of our consciousness. In this context it is also worth mentioning the thinking of Joseph Pieper[29] who proposes that in our technocratic world it is precisely leisure which by force has become our greatest necessity. Surely we need food and shelter, but we also need leisure, for in its own sake there lies a virtue: that of giving us back our capacity for introspection and spirituality.

> The most critical and urgent action we could possibly undertake in today's disintegrating human world would be the establishment, first in ourselves and then in our

settings, of a genuine attitude of faithful leisure, philosophical reflection, and a passionate love for "the truth, the whole truth, and nothing but the truth."

I have been reviewing what we could do for ourselves collectively in light of the ideal which Totila Albert called *El Tres Veces Nuestro* or *Our Three*. In the course of these considerations I have focused on how we must recognize not only the political value of individual transformation, but its necessity, and I have pointed to what a sufficiently strong and wise government could do to promote a generalized awakening of consciousness by underwriting activities which further both the therapeutic and spiritual values in the culture. I have not mentioned, however, the endeavor which might well constitute the activity of greatest promise in the efforts of such a powerful and wise government: an efficient holistic education.

Today education in America is in crisis, yet the response of the establishment to this crisis reveals a striking lack of insight into the true nature of the problem—which is no other than the obsolescence of patriarchal education and its emotional rejection on the part of its choiceless consumers. Current insistence in upgrading standards on the "three R's" and labeling those who reject such diet as psychopathic reflects determination to have education serve mammon rather than man—i.e., national economic growth rather than individual growth. I hope our specialists become wise enough to understand why today's reluctant students cannot "stomach" this even though they may not have the clarity to explain why.

The excessively intellectual and academic training imparted by present universities in their departments of education may become only one of the ingredients in the kind of education we now so urgently need: education that, beyond merely transmitting information, aims to develop complete human beings—without neglecting most specially, attention to the deepest aspects of their being. One may ask who may be able to carry out a work so different from that which has been the offering of current educational institutions. In the last chapter of this book it is the new shamans that we have proposed as our most precious resource. By recruiting some among those who have chosen as vocation the path of personal transformation and have acquired the most effective skills for helping others, our fossilized educational institution, I think, could be effectively transformed. I believe that just as Buckminster Fuller has said that we do not lack the indispensable natural and technological resources, we may say that neither do we lack the necessary human resources, which are at hand.

Before moving on, I want to make reference to a subject that we could collectively support through our understanding and consensus, something that has become very common today as a result of the concerted efforts of small groups—*therapeutic and spiritual communities.* (It is difficult to separate these two aspects when one examines the nature of their aims.) The subject goes beyond therapy and spirituality in view of its educational potential and its significance as political experimentalism.

Indeed, it would be too much of a luxury in the midst of the crisis of our obsolete patriarchal institutions to permit ourselves to merely dream about alternative worlds without actively experimenting with them. Particularly in view of the great failure of the world's socialist experiment as an effective way to achieve a world without government, money or the abuse of power, we must know how to appreciate the valuable contribution entailed in each experimental effort made by "utopian" communities. It is true that many of the "communes" that proliferated during the height of the counterculture in the sixties and seventies have over time disintegrated for a variety of reasons (ranging from the disillusionment of overly optimistic members who dreamed that an alternative way of relating would be so very easy on the one hand, to a "swinging of the pendulum" from idealism to disappointed realism that participants in the early community experienced, and a renewed concern with down-to-earth survival issues, and the exploration of inner work in the world of mainstream society). But I think that the degree of difficulty that many had in living in community was not only due to lack of good faith, having chosen a mistaken path or the severity of the character disorders; for the pressures of the surrounding patriarchal world could well have been less in a society aware of the precious contribution of creative group-life explorations to society, and under a government that interested itself in supporting their development.

I prefer not to give the impression that I have exhausted the subject. Rather I would leave my readers with the invitation to seek out additional corollaries to the idea, establishing new bridges of insight between the visible surface of our problem-complex and the suggested patriarchal core-problem, as well as bridges between the ideal of a tri-une society and relevant items among our resources—such as the conflict resolution techniques (see as described in *The Great Turning*[30]) that are being used in view of an "education for peace" or the political potential of family systems therapy. I only want to add, as an ending, that as we set out to plan and think about how the world could be, we should bear in mind that the world will surely be different from what we are able to conceive. That is to say, that more important than (and beyond) our thoughts and intuitions we need to open ourselves to an emerging creativity. Let me elaborate further through two Biblical images. One, the tower of Babel—symbol of Nimrod—like all conquering human desire to build "titanically" from the bottom to the top, from the known to the unknown. The other, and opposite in St. John's Apocalypse, which describes how after a critical catastrophe, the heavenly Jerusalem descends onto the earth in the form of a cube. This idea of the heavenly city in the shape of a cube, an image crystalline in its exact and divinely organized structure, conveys the intuition and experience of a structure intrinsic to nature that emerges when we get out of the way and become prepared to *receive it*. Just as grace at the individual level may only be received and not produced, so also in collective terms, we must be open and permeable to something beyond our own planning. And because we need to be open, we must be wary of dogmatism and grandiosity with regard to our ideas and our own intelligence.

In conclusion, I want to emphasize that just as ancient spiritual traditions put forth an ethic of work on self towards personal salvation, now such an ethic of self-development begins to be something required of us in terms of *collective* significance too. It is as if the circumstances required the awakening and development within each one of us of that which Buddhism calls "Bodhicitta" and regards a first step on the ladder of enlightenment: the intention of realizing the absolute for the sake of the world.

"Even the least knowledge of things superior is of greater value than the most extensive knowledge of things inferior."
　　　　　　　　　　　THOMAS AQUINAS

"The educational systems of the majority of countries are going through a crisis and rarely do they satisfy existing needs. In actuality we need to define other objectives and other priorities."
　　　　　ALEXANDER KING AND BERTRAND SCHNEIDER[1]

"Human history increasingly becomes a race between education and catastrophe."
　　　　　　　　　　　H. G. WELLS[2]

EDUCATING THE WHOLE PERSON FOR THE WHOLE WORLD

I have proposed that the cure for patriarchal-mindedness needs to be essentially internal, and it behooves our society to take its own inner development in hand. I will here undertake to elaborate on how the inner division and imbalance implied by the patriarchal order calls for a new emphasis and a radically different approach to education.

Let me begin by remarking that the cure is already at our doorstep, together with the disease—for ours is not only a time of patriarchal (and educational) crisis, but a time of *holism*.

There is much talk today of a "shifting paradigm" in science, and, more generally, in our understanding of world and person. What is the emerging paradigm that the new physics invokes as much as contemporary psychology and which, more or less implicitly grasped, is affecting practically every field of understanding and endeavor?

We may call this whole-centered approach "holism" or "integralism." It is the common perspective underlying such diverse inspirations as general systems science and the systems approach to management, gestalt psychology and structuralism. The landmark of our intellectual age is a new appreciation of pattern, organization, the interrelationship of parts in a whole. Life and the universe itself appear to us today as an evolving meta-pattern.

Some two thousand years ago Buddha told the story of blind men who conceive an elephant according to the part of it that they touch, and liken it to a palm tree, a rope, a fan, and so on. This story, revived by the Sufis, has become popular today, and understandably so: it expresses the latest blossom on our *zeitgeist*, the increasingly generalized understanding that the whole is, indeed, more than the sum of the parts.

The shift in our understanding is no doubt the reflection of a living process: if in the intellectual domain ours is an age of holism, more generally speaking, it is an age of synthesis. Not only are we becoming more interdisciplinary, ecumenical and intercultural; we are thirsty to become increasingly unified *persons* in a unified world.

Holistic education, like the holistic approach to things in general, is an aspect of the ongoing synthesis. It was Rousseau—father of romanticism and grandfather of the French Revolution—who first made a plea for the education of feelings. Then a number of others, including Dewey, Maria Montessori and Piaget, emphasized learning through doing. Steiner, and the Waldorf Schools that derived from his work, on the other hand, lay accent on the development of intuition and on what we now call transpersonal education. The human potential movement, more recently, inspired experiments in an education of "the affective domain." Holistic education wants to put all these voices together as it purports to address the whole person: body, feelings, intellect and spirit.

Beyond being holistic in the sense of educating the whole person, however, I think that education should be holistic in other regards as well: in the pursuit of an integration of knowledge, in an orientation toward intercultural integration, a planetary view of things, a balance between theory and practice, the proper taking into account of the future along with the past and present, for instance; because of this, I have felt inclined to use the label *"integral* education" in reference to the emerging educational holism that I personally embrace.

Since we moved in America from the "consciousness revolution" of the sixties to the new conservatism of the eighties, the ideas of an integrated and comprehensive education may meet with the question of some as to whether this is not a luxury. Without addressing himself to education specifically, for instance, Yankelovich writes in the recently published book, *New Rules*,[3] that the world situation is becoming so critical and the individual situation will become so difficult that it is no longer the time for seeking self-fulfillment. The days of the human potential movement, he proposes, should be looked upon as the past reflection of transitory affluence.

I think that we should be on guard against this view, which is nothing but a regression to the hard-nosed attitude which seriously contributed to our present *problematique*. It is precisely the urgency of the *problems* confronting us as a species that makes a new approach to education an imperative, and not a luxury. As Botkin, et al. state in their report to The Club of Rome, *No Limits to Learning*,[4] "After a decade of discussing global issues, small signs of a shift are evident in the debates. Most of the participants engaged in the world simulation modeling and the extensive world conferences have sensed that the dialogues were lacking a critical element. A preoccupation with the material side of the world problematique has limited their scope and effectiveness. Now a new concern has become evident—to restore the human being to the center of the world issues. This suggests a move beyond regarding global issues as manifestations of physical problems in the life-support system, and towards an acceptance of the preeminent importance of the human side of these issues."

The above-quoted writers speak of a "human gap"—the distance between growing complexity and our capacity to cope with it—and claim that this gap may be bridged by learning. "Learning is in this sense far more than just another global problem: its failure represents, in a fundamental way, the issue of issues in the world problematique." In sum, "Learning has become a life-and-death matter."

My own preference is to emphasize "development," and to say that unless our larval nature turns into the next stage in our metamorphosis we can be expected to wreck our environment and greedily destroy one another. The transformation that all ages have known as possible for a human is not a potential that we can afford to neglect any further; what was the destiny of a few and may have seemed a luxury in the past now presents itself as a collective emergency. For as our mistakes are amplified by our power and the consequences thereof become inescapable as a result of population growth, we cannot fail to see that they are the expression of an incompletely developed psyche.

We have known for a long time now that the psychology of the average human—that psychology which we call "normal"—is, psychoanalytically speaking, regressive. Under a layer of pseudo-abundance we are dissatisfied, dependent and voracious. Would our world's annual military expenditure be what it is if we were not an unconsciously paranoid and cannibalistic society? Would it not be reasonable to devote such a sum, rather, to an earth-repair program extending from ecology to consciousness-raising?

Early in our collective life we experienced the hardship of the ice ages and that of the desiccation of the earth that followed. These were at the same time challenges that spurred us on in an evolution, and traumas that precipitated us into "a fall," a psychosocial pathology. Deficiency-motivation—with its consequent exploitation of others, nature and ourselves—has perpetuated itself through contagion, infecting our psyche through the generations, and now is bringing us to the brink of a shipwreck from which we may only be saved if we know how to swim. "Swimming" in this metaphor stands for the new consciousness that is our birthright, and may take us from "here" to "there": from our obsolete and centuries-old conditioning to a new world order.

Far from being a luxury, a new education—an education of the whole person for the whole world—is both an urgent need and our greatest hope, for all our problems would be utterly simplified if we first achieved true sanity, and the ability to love that is part of it. Individual peace cannot be dispensed with as a basis for world peace.

Many of those who read this may be part of the generation of seekers that has prompted some to speak of our times as the dawn of a "New Age"—a movement of renewal comparable to that at the dawn of Christianity, or that at the rise of other world religions. This cultural phenomenon, which exploded in the U.S. about thirty years ago, has gone through an upbeat of excitement and a downbeat of burnout, and may be said to echo the structure of a psychological process: after the well-known enthusiasm of entering the path—when it seemed that the whole world would soon be transformed—a considerable portion of the population proceeded to the equally well-known stage of realizing that (as Gurdjieff used to put it) "at the beginning it is roses, roses, later it is thorns, thorns." A whole generation embarked on the quest, practically speaking; yet the outcome has not been, thus far, a transformed society, but a number of would-be shamans in different stages of development: partially transformed individuals who have something to contribute from their experience and who now know that the journey is much harder and longer than what they thought.

If the transformation of an adult is so difficult, it may be easier to start with the young. If we think from the perspective of the whole and the needs of our living earth, eduation—and, particularly, assistance to the *growth* of the individual during the time of greater plasticity—stands out as the best strategy by which we may consciously intervene in our evolutionary transformation. It is certainly the most economic one, at a time when economy has become critical.

Hitler once discovered that by controlling education it was possible to control society. Monstrous as his conception was, it was the echo of a *caricatured* great truth, and we can retrieve the truth of the matter by standing his proposition on its head—for it is not through "control" that our aim may be accomplished, but by attention, skill, warmth and the quality of our own being. Yet it is through education of the young to full humanness that we may expect a better world. If we come to "control" education, we need to understand well, however, that this will need to be a control in the service of liberation—a sort of counter-control (much as meditation is a "voluntary control" of internal states that aims at deep spontaneity and noninterference).

We are all acquainted with the expression, "educating the men the country needs." What has been meant by it has been, in general, education as socialization, i.e., education as a vehicle of social conditioning. If we now speak of educating the people that the *world* needs, we must understand that the process will necessarily be not an education for conformity but for freedom and autonomy—for only on the basis of true individuals may there be a true "world."

Herbert Spencer, writing after Darwin, compared society to an organism. Perhaps the criticism that his idea received from later social scientists reflected the fact that *our* society is not much like an organism, and that in this we are not so advanced as the bees and the ants. A society that is more like a brain to the individual nerve cells would first have to rest upon the existence of mature humans—this necessarily implies integrated and self-realizing humans—rather than the humanlike robots that generalized blindness and "ills of society" have traditionally encouraged.

It may be said that an education for individual wholeness is in itself an education for the larger whole, "an education for the whole world," and yet I have wanted to emphasize this idea of an "education for the whole world" (by including it in the title of this chapter) firstly, to emphasize the thesis that "an education of the whole person *is* an education for the whole world"; also, because it may be salutary to emphasize the meta-personal goal. And inspiring: if we are aware of how much we need an education for peace and an education for world unity, this is likely to lead us to the corresponding creative contributions.

An individual cannot be truly whole without a sense of the whole world, a sense of brotherhood. We need an education that brings the individual to that point of maturity when he or she rises from the perspective of isolated self-hood and tribal-mindedness to the fully developed sense of community that can serve as an experimental foundation to a planetary perspective. I think it is important to emphasize this today since we are seeing the beginning of an attention to an education in ecology and what we need to do to live in a sustainable world. Yet, the emphasis thus far is (patriarchally) moralistic and cognitive. An education of the self-as-part-of-humankind is neglected: an education of the sense of humanity.

The spiritual birth that is part of our potential destiny is not the birth of the "I" only, but the birth of a "Thou." The birth of Being is, more exactly speaking, the birth of I-Thou, the birth of we-ness, relatedness.

How can education contribute to a we-sense? Not only through a nonparochial attitude and whole-earth view of things, but most importantly, through skilled community leadership: i.e., the skilled assistance of the process of group formation in the true sense of the term.

Carl Rogers has said in our age of nuclear physics and cybernetics that "groups" may be the most significant invention of our century. The future will tell. They are certainly a great resource, and I think teachers should acquire the skill in facilitating honest communication and dealing with its consequences, in being able to recognize and express one's experience, developing empathy, encountering others genuinely and staying away from ego-games. The process should not be restricted to encounter group meetings and the like, however, but (as George Brown has appropriately pointed out) it should constitute a background and context to the teaching situation. There are two kinds of groups that represent particularly important forms of community activity and which I want to highlight: one is the task-group, which provides the ideal situation for learning collaboration and for developing an awareness of its impediments; the other, the decision-making group, which offers a peculiarly revealing mirror for individual character and I think it could afford us an unequalled resource toward an education for democracy if turned into an opportunity for self-knowledge with the assistance of psychodynamically skilled facilitators.

In applying such resources we must bear in mind that growth is inseparable from healing; only artificially can we divorce the provinces of education, psychotherapy, and the spiritual disciplines, for in truth there is a single process of growth-healing-enlightenment. The taboo about bringing psychotherapy into education needs to be seen for the regressive and defensive symptom that it is; without dealing with the affective domain in education we will continue to have a world with all-too-many individuals fixed in childish patterns of behavior, feeling and thinking, and it would be preposterous to imagine that we can achieve the goal of personal growth.

After having said in so many words that integral education is an idea whose time has come, let me now share something of my view as to what an education of the future might look like. As I set out to do this, I cannot fail to remember Aldous Huxley's essay on the subject, "On the Education of an Amphibian."[5] My observations and suggestions will unavoidably constitute an update to his pioneering invitation to a holistic education about forty years ago.

Needless to say, the new education will address itself to body and emotions, mind and spirit. But how, and with what tools?

In regard to physical education we know enough by now to recognize that aside from physical fitness training and sports there is a subtler type of bodywork. This is the domain of what Dr. Thomas Hanna called "the new somatologies." We might speak of an outer and inner bodywork—just as these words have been applied to sports. What needs to be added to traditional physical education is the question of attitude and attention, and, in addition, it would be advisable to incorporate into the curriculum some forms of sensory-motor training. Not only are the contributions from the modern bodywork movement such as the Feldenkrais movements and Gerda Alexander's Eutonia appropriate and excellent, but old approaches such as hatha-yoga and tai chi chuan are as well.

Another domain that needs to be given attention—in regard to the physical aspect of the human *holon*—is that of skillful *doing*, as it is involved in housekeeping, cooking and crafts. Just as psychopathology interferes with the ability to mobilize oneself in view of a task, the cultivation of a healthy attitude toward one's activity is psychotherapeutic. Manual labor is also the occasion for the development of profound virtues such as patience and contentedness—if we only are guided into the understanding of the inner side of crafts—i.e., the use of the outer situation for one's inner growth as a person (concerning which more can be learned from the Sufi tradition, for instance, than from occupational therapy).

Let us move on to the education of feelings. First of all, it needs to be said that it would be artificial to separate what belongs to "affective education" and to the education of interpersonal relations; likewise, we cannot quite separate the affective interpersonal domain from the issue of self-knowledge. Thus, it is under the rubric of interpersonal education that I want to remark that self-knowledge, self-study, self-understanding—that high ideal that Socrates ardently espoused and recommended—is most neglected in today's educational venture, at a time when we have the resources to make it otherwise. It is high time that our curricula included a modernly conceived laboratory in which self-understanding is pursued and facilitated in a context of interpersonal awareness and the training of communicative capacity—bringing together the many resources that have become available since Freud introduced the exercise of free association and particularly including the latest refinements in the humanistic movement.

Of course we need to develop, if not recover, the ability to know our feelings and to authentically express them when appropriate. Furthermore, we cannot afford to exclude the contribution of dramatization and, more generally, expression, to the development of feeling life. A resource of liberal education here is important in this regard: exposure to the world's literary and artistic heritage under the appropriate guidance, for art is an inheritance of the human heart through the heart, just as science and philosophy are an inheritance of the mind through the mind.

The most important thing that I have to say in regard to what affective domain education could be, however, is that we need to acknowledge the development of love as its central aim.

There can be no doubt that sanity and its concomitant natural virtue are inseparable from the ability to love oneself and others. Accordingly, we need a pedagogy of love. We have enough information to develop such a pedagogy; perhaps what has been lacking is a sense of direction and the occasion to apply it in an education setting. We know, for instance, that in addition to warmth, understanding and psychological safety, and in addition to the occasion to develop a sense of community, it is necessary to deal with the childish ambivalence that most people growing up in our society develop as an inevitable reaction to less than emotionally mature, happy, and productive parents. A person's potential to love is veiled over by self-hate and conscious or unconscious destructiveness, and these have arisen from early life history. To be free from these, psychotherapeutic experience has shown clearly enough by now, it is necessary to reexamine one's life to the point of more than intellectual insight, and to ventilate the pain and frustration associated with past impressions before these can be dropped. Of course these things are done in the course of deep psychotherapy over an extended time, but they may be accomplished far more briefly today than in the days of psychoanalytic exploration.

In the world of humanistic psychology, perhaps the resource which has been most systematically explored in view to its integration to the educational context—at least in the United States—has been the gestalt approach (under the name of "confluent education"). George Brown, professor of education at the Santa Barbara campus of the University of California and a gestaltist as well, received the support of both the Esalen Institute and the Ford Foundation already 20 years ago, and has been seriously providing gestalt education for teachers, not with the intent of making gestalt therapy an additional part of the curriculum, but so as to give teachers a greater capacity to comprehend experiential truth, increased ability to understand the human condition and to handle themselves as persons in the face of other persons and thus working at the interface between therapy and instruction. I believe that Gestalt deserves to be recommended as a primary resource in terms of its economics: a *brief* exposure to Gestalt can give a person that type of capacity because it offers the individual an increased ability to be in the here-and-now. Most people live under an implicit taboo against the expression of what is happening with them in the moment, so that when one acquires the capacity to be more aware and to take responsibility for one's experience in the here-and-now a thousand new things can happen; it is a liberation from which derive many consequences. When one can interrupt what is happening at the level of intellectual discourse and say, for instance, "I smell a rat," or "This makes me uncomfortable," or "I am becoming bored with this situation," thus shifting toward the interpersonal level, much sterility and stagnation can be overcome.

What I have said of Gestalt therapy can apply, more or less, to Transactional Analysis, psychodrama and other contemporary therapies. They deserve to be considered as a part of a mosaic of resources that would contribute both to the personal development of educators and to the improvement in their professional skills.

Yet as I consider the future possibilities of education and the resources that it might bring into its arena, I want to specially emphasize the great educational potential of an approach that did not originate in the professional world, but rather in the spiritual, and which I see as ideally fitting for inclusion in high school curricula and of great relevance to our patriarchal ills; for it is specifically oriented toward an integration of the inner "father," "mother" and "child" sub-personalities within the person. It is known as the "Quadrinity Process," for its ambition is one of harmonizing body, emotions, intellect and spirit.

More than ten years ago, at the second Gestalt Conference in Baltimore, I recommended this method (then known as the Fischer-Hoffman Process) as something very appropriate for the training of gestaltists and as a resource for the education of therapists in general. Many issues are made explicit through the "Process" (as it is sometimes called for short) that are relevant to psychotherapeutic training, but I believe that the great potential of the approach is educational. Its focus is a person's relationships with his/her parents, living or dead, and its underlying idea is, I think, the same that accounts for the importance of the fourth commandment: just as unlove toward parents disturbs a person's relationships to self and world in general, the reestablishment of the loving bond to parents (a loving bond which most people do not even suspect they have lost) can reestablish the possibility of another level of love toward oneself and, by extension, toward others. Since the great educational potential of this new approach to the healing of internalized father-mother-child relationships is a vital ingredient in this book, I speak about it at length in the next chapter.

The other side of an education of love is the transpersonal or spiritual. One half of what we can do is the undoing of the "ego," the transcendence of character, the process of liberation from our fetters; the other side, the cultivation of those qualities that are the aim of meditation; for as is well known and is the message of every great religion, love flows naturally from mystical experience. The subject of meditation, too, I leave for a later portion of this chapter.

I believe that the neglect of affective education has been mostly due to taboo against therapy in the world of education. Just as in the case of religion, there is a feeling that the province of education should be separate and should not be confused by the therapeutic. There is a somewhat territorial consideration involved here, but also understandable considerations that have not been confronted or evaluated in an appropriate spirit; complications such as arise when a child at school begins to speak about what happens at home. It is common for parents to feel uncomfortable, and conflict arises between the therapeutic desirability of ventilation and their wish for privacy. I do not think that these are things that can be managed at the local level alone, and that the teachers and school administrators need higher support or directives if they are to take initiatives of importing into the schools some of the methodology available for emotions healing. If the world crisis that is affecting us is a crisis in the realm of relationships—a crisis arising from a limited capacity for love—it is absurd that we permit ourselves to continue making that obsolete separation between the therapeutic and the educational.

It might be expected that less would need to be said or done about the cognitive side of education than about other aspects, since cognitive content is that upon which education has focused almost exclusively until now. Yet the intellectual aspect of education needs to be much more than the transmission of information—whether this be toward the goal of understanding the world or of being able to perform specialized work in it. And once we envision bringing into education more than cognitive content, as I am suggesting, this confronts us with a need to carry out the informational aspect of schooling much more efficiently than it has thus far been done—simply because we will have less time for it. We need to take advantage of the full potential of puzzles and games (the ideal medium for the early learning of mathematics), to deploy our audio-visual resources, to explore the possibilities of computers, and so on. But above all, we need, I think, what I call an ethics of brevity. We cannot afford to load up the storage capacity of our brains with piecemeal information of nonessential meaning, but must concentrate on meaningfulness—either in terms of a worldview or in terms of vocation and preparation for service. The thirst for understanding is part of human nature and needs to be fed with a panoramic contemplation of knowledge. It would be wise therefore to carry out an education that entails a balance of generalism and specialization; that is, one that provides specialized skills on a background of general content. This in itself would imply some education of integrative thinking.

What today's perspective shows as not sufficiently emphasized in traditional education is the developing of cognitive skills beyond learning content. We need, in addition to learning, and above all, to learn how to learn. Even if we adopt a pragmatic rather than a humanistic attitude, we must come to this conclusion. "The amount of knowledge that one acquires of a content area is generally unrelated to superior performance in an occupation," writes Professor Kilpatrick in the bulletin of AHHP. "Most occupations require only that an individual be willing and able . . . It is neither the acquisition of knowledge nor the use of knowledge that distinguishes the outstanding performer but rather the cognitive skills that are developed and exercised in the process of acquiring and using knowledge."

Here too, we need to shift our focus from the outer to the inner, from the apparent to the subtle.

There are new resources that education could draw upon today for the nurturing of cognitive skills, such as de Bono's lateral thinking exercises, training in the examination of assumptions (see, for instance, Abercrombie[6] and Mayfield[7]), dialectical thinking, Feuerstein's nonverbal education of general intelligence, and so on. Yet I want to linger upon two that are not new, yet must not be forgotten. Firstly, mathematics. This is a content area of extraordinary value in the education of reasoning itself, as the education of the past has understood well. If we aspire to a right-left brain balance, let us beware of throwing mathematics overboard as an academic exercise of the past, as our right-brained subculture seems to feel inclined. Secondly, music. All creative expression through any medium may be approached as a means of developing intuition, yet music stands out among them in this regard in a way equivalent to the way mathematics stands out among the sciences. Music is "sensuous mathematics" as Polyani has said, and that can do for our intuitive brain what mathematics does for our reasoning hemisphere. In this regard we may have something to learn from the Hungarians who, under the direction of Zoltan Kodaly some two decades ago, have been pioneers in musical education and have observed its beneficial consequences on children in terms of measured intelligence. There are special resources available in this domain, too, upon which our schools could draw—such as the Orf system and Dalcroze's eurythmics.

We come now to the topic of transpersonal education—i.e., the education of that aspect of the person which lies beyond body, feelings, and intellect, and which has traditionally been referred to as "spirit." Let me brooch the subject by addressing myself first of all to the controversial issue of whether religion is to be taught or not in the classroom. Once religion was compulsory; later, secular education claimed its independence from the church—and this was a step forward in the unfolding of modern society. But was not the baby thrown out with the bathwater? One thing is independence from the authority of a specific religious hierarchy, and another the issue of spiritual education. The religious domain is an aspect of human nature and no education can call itself holistic and leave it unattended. Yet the spirit of the age is no longer compatible with the inculcation of dogma nor with a provincial attitude: the time has come for a trans-systemic and transcultural approach to the realm of spirit. As I once heard the late Bishop Myers saying, "We cannot any longer afford not to familiarize ourselves with the whole human heritage." What we need is obviously a "religion class" that would present the essence of the spiritual teachings of the world, and that would underline the common human experience that they symbolize, interpret, and cultivate in different ways.

Next, I want to bring up the issue of *when* to expose a child to religious education. There are practices of spiritual significance suitable for children that may be regarded as meditation equivalents, such as exposure to nature, arts, crafts, dance, bodywork, and most importantly, story-telling and guided fantasy. Yet, in my view, the ideal time for the beginnings of an explicit spiritual education is that of puberty and not earlier, unless our aim is brainwashing. Primitive cultures—which as we know today may be spiritually sophisticated—typically introduce their members to the symbols and revelations of their tradition on occasion of a rite of passage, an initiation into adolescence and adulthood. Before then, religious issues are treated as mysteries for which there will be a time and appropriate guidance. I think there is wisdom in this widespread practice, for it is in adolescence that the passion for metaphysical understanding makes itself felt, turning many teenagers into natural philosophers. And, most importantly, adolescence coincides with the beginning of longing, the awakening of the energy that moves the seeker along the quest. This, therefore, is the biologically appropriate time to tell the growing person of the journey and its goal, about helpers, vehicles, tools, and talismans.

Needless to say, a spiritual education should not remain theoretical—though the spiritual teachings constitute a suitable context for the practices. If there is going to be a "religion class" in the curriculum, it should be coupled to an experiential introduction to the spiritual disciplines, a "religion lab" that would comprise instructions in meditation and related practices, and provide the individual who leaves school with the basic tools for advancing spiritually in daily life.

Time will elapse before duly trained individuals may be available to implement an experiential course in the spiritual disciplines from a transcultural and integral perspective. Before then, our best option may be that of offering students a "tasting" period with a choice among the chief spiritual disciplines of the world—for which guides are available. I think that in the future we may have occasion to implement a trans-systemic program of spiritual exercises conceived according to the natural and objective components of spiritual training and aspects of the psychospiritual process upon which they converge. It is clear, for instance, that a natural beginning for such a program would be concentration practice—for upon the ability to concentrate rest all forms of meditation, prayer and worship.

Even though I resist the temptation to deal at length with this subject—which constitutes one of my specialities—I will only say succinctly that I conceive the existing forms of spiritual practice as either pure forms or combinations of a limited number of "internal actions," and I believe that we should seek to cultivate these different "psychological gestures" just as in physical education we exercise the different movement possibilities of the body. For the optimized consciousness that all spiritual disciplines have as a goal is a many-faceted condition and experience, wherein are fused qualities of clarity, calm, freedom, nonattachment, love and numinosity. And though the cultivation of each of these constitutes a path by itself, there is something to be gained by an integrative approach which aims, beyond these qualities, at the ineffable goal upon which they converge.

In addition to effectiveness, the advantage of a program conceived upon an understanding of the underlying dimensions of spiritual practice would lead to the experiential conciliation of many paradoxes and the end of narrow-minded debate as to "the true way." A by-product of it would be a spontaneous understanding of the essentials of all traditions.

I have accomplished my task of envisioning the components and resources of what I call an integral education: an education of body, feelings, mind and spirit, that is comprehensive and balanced, and brings into the world beings cognizant of and generously inclined toward it. What can we *do* about this noble enterprise?

Of course the decisive thing is the growth and diffusion of understanding. Progress of understanding on the part of all is likely to lead to more creative developments than what we have seen in the private school domain—and that is something.

The next step toward the implementation of the dream, however, lies in the education of educators.

This is already taking place, to a limited extent, in the form of the self-directed continuing education of many teachers who for the sake of their own growth or their work are seeking and finding the necessary experiences and information. It is to be hoped, however, that before long the schools of education may embrace enough of the holistic understanding that by the time of leaving the university teachers will have developed the perspective and skills, maturity and depth that a total education requires. For life only proceeds from life, and maturation only from ripened people, above all when the issue is this strictly human formation.

What is missing from current schools of education is to give teachers both therapeutic and spiritual abilities, and all these could well be included in schools of education in a relatively economical way. (I say this from experience, as I have carried out brief intensive programs with such ingredients with excellent results.) At present, students of education receive an excess of intellectual baggage and an insufficient emotional and spiritual education; for example, in psychology a lot is learned about behaviorism and not a single thing that helps to change *people;* that is to say, they learn about changing discrete behaviors, but not much about how to change life. Why? Because behaviorism is *scientific,* it only deals with things that can be measured.

Once, one of my professors at medical school, Ignacio Matte-Blanco, a Chilean psychoanalyst who migrated many years ago to Italy, told me about a friend of his who had wanted to study medicine because his vocation was the human being— to understand the human mind. In time, he came to realize how far anybody was from being able to pursue a true science of the mind, and in the end he dedicated his life to the study of the transmission of nervous impulses and the polarization of the membrane of the cuttlefish's axon. I believe that something of this has happened to all of us; by virtue of being scientists we have limited the range of our interests to that which science can measure and has come to include—and thus we have fallen prey to the patriarchal game of scientism, which is, of course, not the same as science, but a caricature of the scientific spirit.

Educational reform within the government-sponsored school system will come naturally from the diffusion and ripening of awareness in the population, and particularly among the professionals. Today's revolution is tomorrow's establishment. Social institutions have their characteristic inertia, and growth results from the overpowering of inertia by vision— "the taming power of the small." The inertia of the educational establishment has earned it the appropriate comparison with a white elephant, and the obsoleteness and irrelevancy of what service it provides at present is unconscionable. I have no doubt that school refractoriness is a reaction to it. We may understand it as a sort of schooling strike of protest against irrelevancy, a plea for an education relevant to our critical times and real issues before us, a plea for an education that might truly be called wise and truly help us to become better.

I hope to convey some sense of the destructiveness and irrelevance of our present anti-holistic, patriarchal system of education with respect to our real human situation, and will also communicate that this is something that deserves urgent attention. Our education is as absurd as it is potentially "salvific." So absurd that many have spoken of dismantling the schools as the most adequate solution (Ivan Illich has seen the dismantling of the schools as a fundamental step toward a great liberation that we need from the authoritarian form in general). Many believe that contemporary education has not only failed to accomplish its function, but also by default, harmed us. I think, as I write this, of a photomontage in which one could see the picture of a group of very lively children next to another of robot-faced and bored people riding a street car, with the caption reading, "What has happened?"

If I speak of "urgency" and not just of relevance, I do it in view of our global situation. At the same time in which we are living through a crisis attributable to a failing in human relationships, interpersonal learning is completely neglected.

After many years during which the expression "world problematique" has circulated in reference to our macroproblem, Alexander King, cofounder of The Club of Rome, has in his recently published book, *The First World Revolution*,[8] coined the new term "resolutics." He emphasizes in his view of our way out (along with technology) education. He asserts that education should embrace the following goals:

- to acquire knowledge;

- to structure intelligence and develop the critical faculties;

- to develop knowledge of oneself and of one's consciousness and of one's own capacities and limitations;
- to learn to overcome undesirable impulses and destructive behavior;
- to awaken permanently the creative and imaginative faculties in each person;
- to learn to exercise a responsible role in the life of society;
- to learn to communicate with others;
- to help people to adapt to and prepare for change;
- to permit each person the acquisition of a global vision of the world;
- to shape people such that they can be operative and capable of resolving problems.

I celebrate his statement, and yet feel that something vital is lost in a language of pure objectivity borrowed from economics, politics and engineering. It is significant that the words "love" and "compassion" are absent. They are implicitly forbidden words in our sinister-brained phallocratic* world, just as it was in bad taste to mention the incubator among the test-tube people in Aldous Huxley's brave new world. And I don't think the language issue is trivial—for we need feeling language to address a feeling issue. Perhaps the matter of environmental education, which has received more attention than the restoration of the human capacity to love can illustrate my emphasis, for the levels of population and overconsumption that we have reached have turned the matter of garbage (nuclear waste included) critical to our survival. Educators

---

*I borrow the word from Mary Daly in *Gyn/Ecology*.

have caught on to the fact that ecology constitutes a "soft technology" that may work against the devastation of unmitigated industrialism, yet a "care" of the environment inspired by the understanding that we need to act in this or that way (i.e., a care contingent on a selfish combination of intelligence and practicality) may not be enough.

I believe that such an attitudinal change is necessary that cannot be divorced from "reasons of the heart"—as is the case among American Indians, whose culture is permeated by an atmosphere of felt solidarity with the earth and brotherhood with all its creatures, an altruistic love of nature for *itself* that can hardly be the experience of one who (in view of childhood problems with parents) is not even capable of loving himself or herself or other human beings truly.

I imagine that a reaction similar to mine in face of a purely pragmatic environmentalism and pacifism has inspired the slogan that I recently saw in a sticker on a car window: "practice random kindness and senseless acts of beauty."

Perhaps a serious reason for the lack of further progress in the very formulation of these additional tasks of education is an implicit notion that it would be exceedingly expensive to implement them. For it is only natural to think that such a radical shift in education's goals—to say nothing of its means—would involve a corresponding shift in personnel. Yet I think this is a revolution that would be within our reach—provided that there is sufficient awareness. At the time of the French Revolution, a radical change in orientation (from humanistic education to scientific education) was carried out because there was a strong government endorsing it, and the authorities envisioning the desirability of a hitherto nonexistent scientific education took the initiative of importing scientists from the laboratories into the schools.

I believe that now we could do something comparable: give a limited place to the subjects that currently constitute instruction (for truly the greatest part of what we learn, we learn outside of school), condense much of what is currently being done in schools, and bring into schools—schools of education, included—people who have been occupying themselves with their own inner/higher development—people within the growing experiential therapeutic and spiritual movement.* I believe that it is within this broad movement that are to be found those who can assist the present generation of educators, and educational administrators will do well in recruiting them in a visiting capacity—at least in connection with the training of the holistic educators of tomorrow. For just as life only proceeds from life, also ripeness can be best furthered by the ripe.

---

*It happens that our times of educational impoverishment are also times of therapeutic and spiritual enrichment since the rise of that post-Freudian cultural wave, aspects of which have been called the human potential movement, humanistic psychology, transpersonal psychology and the consciousness revolution.

"Honor your father and your mother so that you may have a long life in the land that Yahweh your God has given you."
EXODUS 20,12

"It is natural that the gods forgive those who honor their parents above all else, for it is through them that we have learned to honor the divine."
JÁMBLICO[1]

"It is a sign of a good man that he loves his father and mother."
G. I. GURDJIEFF[2]

"Religions say that we must forgive the injustice we suffered; only then will we be free to love and be purged of hatred. This is correct as far as it goes, but how do we find the path of the true forgiveness?"
ALICE MILLER[3]

A NEW TOOL FOR THE REEDUCATION OF LOVE

Just as I have dealt in Chapter II with a major aspect of the resolutics in view of the patriarchal world, in this third chapter I elaborate further on one of the resources that I have proposed for a future holistic education.

Together with the "technology of the sacred" of which Theodore Roszak spoke in the sixties, we should surely consider the technologies of the *human* in the purer meaning of the term—pointing, beyond man-the-machine, to the human heart.

A "technology of love"—in particular—(if the expression may be permitted) would be of momentous importance in the fields of both education and psychotherapy; for we surely need a methodology more efficient than what has been available thus far, ranging from traditional religious injunctions to psychoanalysis. I am convinced that the little-known piece of modern pop psychology that I describe below responds to this claim.

The Quadrinity Process that Robert Hoffman introduced in the sixties may be called a pop psychology in the same sense that the Erhard Seminars Training (EST) or mind control groups can: it did not originate within the professional and academic realm, though distinguished professionals like Dr. Hogle at Stanford University, Dr. Knoble at UNICAMP University in Campinas, Brazil, and others have endorsed it enthusiastically. However humble its birth may have been and however naive (in the sense of unschooled) its conception, it may be said to embody some of the main insights of psychoanalysis and valuable practical contributions of humanistic psychology, as I expect to show below.

The Transpersonal Movement today may be said to reflect in psychology a vaster cultural phenomenon: the coming to meet of East and West. It has been largely the spiritual influence of the East on the West that has opened up therapists to the recognition of transpersonal factors. Thus, Jung was strongly appreciative of the Chinese books, *The Golden Flower*, the *I Ching*, and *The Tibetan Book of the Dead*, and later a powerful wave of influence swept the West with Zen, beginning with D. T. Suzuki and followed by Suzuki Roshi's coming to California, the books of Alan Watts in America and of Graf Durkheim in Europe. In contrast to the atmosphere of Eastern, most particularly Buddhist, spirituality in the transpersonal movement, Robert Hoffman's Quadrinity Process stands out as one of two significant exceptions, sharing the background of *Western* spirituality with *The Course in Miracles*, another extra-academic contribution to the transpersonal field.

In the foreword to Bob Hoffman's *No One is to Blame/Getting a Loving Divorce from Mom & Dad*,[4] I had said, "I am happy to believe that I have incurred some good karma by playing John the Baptist in this story." I referred to opening up the way for someone who had much to offer and to my having "baptized" his work with the then current name of "Fischer-Hoffman Process." The John the Baptist image also seemed particularly relevant in view of the Judeo-Christian spirit of Bob Hoffman's work.

Not only does the Quadrinity Process align itself with the central injunction of the Christian gospel to "Love your neighbor as yourself and God above all things," but the way in which Hoffman goes about this therapeutic goal may be said to be an echo of the old Jewish injunction to love and honor one's parents. I think that it makes much sense to consider the love for our parents as guarantee of and a barometer for mental health, because its lays the ground for loving oneself and others. Thus, we may think of the Mosaic commandment as a most important piece of social engineering. With the rise of psychotherapy, however, a possibility has opened up for moving closer to the old aspiration than was possible through ethical rules alone. The method that the Quadrinity Process offers for reestablishing loving relationships with our parents is to the mere admonition to love them just as practical assistance in the reawakening of love is to mere indoctrination concerning the goodness of loving.

Whereas it was enough on occasion of *No One is to Blame* to recommend the author and his book, in these pages I have perceived my task as that of an ambassador or translator from the intuitive world (from which the Quadrinity Process sprang) into the academic world of scientific psychology. It is not so much in a "John the Baptist" role that I find myself then, but (resorting to another quasi-archetypal prototype) in that of a Plato before Socrates.

Though proclaimed by the oracle of Delphi as the wisest man of his time, Socrates was not an intellectual. Neither did he write any books. All this was done by Plato, the theoretician and translator of Socrates to the world of philosophers. Socrates's concern was that of urging and stimulating others to know themselves, and though he challenged faulty reasoning with reason, we always feel in the presence of a wisdom that transcends logical thinking, perhaps the inspiration of what he called his *daimon*. However momentous his influence may have been in the history of philosophy, he did not set out or formulate a theory of the cosmos, man, or the divine.

Psychotherapy in general may be said to be a highly Socratic art. It is, to begin with, an art more than a science, for however useful a theoretical understanding may be for therapeutic practice, psychotherapy is a practice that cannot be properly conducted without intuition. There are therapists who are intuitive and rational at the same time, and whose vocation is (as frequently happens in medicine) both theoretical and philanthropic. Other therapists (and these might be properly called the "Socratic" types) are eminently persons of intuition, whose specific talent lies in their perception of people and whose creativity manifests itself in the interpersonal situation.

Fritz Perls was one such Socratic psychotherapist. His genius lay in therapeutic praxis, not in theory: he was a man of the spoken word more than a writer. (His early books were largely the work of friends and collaborators, while his legacy from later life consisted mostly in the audiotapes and videotapes of his work.) His reliance on intuition was so great that I have proposed to regard him as an embodiment or exemplar of a modern Western "neo-shamanism."

I have been suggesting for years that what is presently called "transpersonal psychology" may be understood as the reflection in psychology of a wider cultural phenomenon that can itself be interpreted as the rise of a new shamanism in the Western world. This new shamanism may be observed in the respiritualization of psychotherapy today, in a growing intuitionism, and a greater reliance of therapists on their individual experience and creativity, as was the case in traditional shamanism, in which each healer carries one's own "bag of tricks," emblematic of the uniqueness of one's path. The new shamanism, like the early one, is a phenomenon of vocation, and it involves, too, the contagion of vocation, such as has recently exploded psychotherapy beyond the professional domain.

Hoffman may be described as a Socratic type and as a Western shaman, for a profound and inwardly guided personal transformation gave him the ability to help others psychologically. As is the case with shamans, his work has emerged from visionary experience and intuition, and he upholds a "magical attitude" in regard to the existence of spirits (human and more than human). Also, he is eminently a man of vocation and not a professional. The fact that he is not very well educated in the intellectual sense only brings him closer to the shaman archetype.

Today the attitude of academia, just like that of the theological and political establishments throughout history, is ambivalent in regard to this rising neo-shamanism. Just as mystics have been a target of criticism from the theologists, and healers have been persecuted by the medical profession, so academic psychology, proud of its intellectual heritage, may look disdainfully upon professionally untrained men of "only" vocation and experience. Thus, some readers of Hoffman's scant writing may not approve of finding that, as psychoanalyst Mauricio Knoble observes in connection with *No One is to Blame*, "The traditional historical background was missing, as well as the scientific background, the theoretical foundation, the experimental data, the statistical validation, and the bibliography." Because such criticism on the part of the psychologically sophisticated reader might get in the way of appreciating and learning from the present book, I hope that I may show that, while the "traditional historical background" has not been known to Hoffman, his work is most congruent with it, as well as with the background of current psychological discourse.

Let me begin by pointing out that Hoffman's "Process," unlike other transpersonal therapies, stands out for its currently psychoanalytic spirit. Transpersonal psychology today is permeated by the anti-psychoanalytic attitude of the humanistic movement, which sprang up largely in reaction to the limitations of psychoanalysis. However, in throwing Freudian and post-Freudian insights overboard in their eagerness to attain "the higher reaches of human nature," are not transpersonalists bypassing an unavoidable segment of the human growth process? Though espousing a holistic attitude in theory, I think that in practice the transpersonal movement conveys a spiritualistic bias that has gone hand in hand with a neglect of the psychodynamic range of experience and healing. In this regard, Hoffman's work is a welcome synthesis. The affinity of the Quadrinity Process with psychoanalysis is striking, and, as may be inferred from what I have already said of Bob Hoffman, the coincidence between his ideas and that of psychoanalysis is *not* the outcome of an influence, but of a naive rediscovery: a fresh foundation of facts about the human mind that are there to be observed by anybody who approaches them with enough depth. Hoffman (to whom Dr. Knoble refers as a person with a "genuine naivete [that is] alarmingly effective") does not even share average information on Freudian psychology. While most educated people share a fair amount of the Freudian inheritance that has seeped beyond professional boundaries into every man's language, Hoffman (once a tailor) seems to have a naivete comparable to that of the painter Henri Rousseau, who was a customs official.

Just as the Judeo-Christian and psychoanalytic orientations are rare in today's transpersonal movement, I regard as rarer still the coming together of these two views: for, on the whole, the psychoanalytic movement has taken sides with antireligious orientation, while spiritually oriented people have responded to psychoanalytic invalidations with analogous criticism, deeming psychoanalysis as a method limited by erroneous assumptions.

It is true that there have been some exceptions to this antireligious bias of psychoanalytic therapists. David Bakan points out that Freud may have derived inspiration from Jewish mysticism, and Bruno Bettelheim claims that English translation has presented Freud in a less spiritual light than he sounds in the original, where, for instance, he frequently uses the word *seele,* soul. Karen Horney is sympathetic to the spiritual perspective, and in the last decades people like Bion, Kohut, and Lacan have in different ways opened up psychoanalysis to the recognition of a nonmechanistic factor in the psyche. Fromm, who in *Man for Himself* contends that the restoration of love to oneself, others, and God is both the basis of happiness and the goal of psychoanalysis, could well be regarded as an intellectual forerunner of the Quadrinity Process.

However, the convergence between Christian and psychoanalytic outlooks in the Quadrinity Process is most significant in regard to two attitudes that mostly continue to be considered incompatible concerning aberrated emotionality. Whereas the traditional perspective has been one of cultivating positive emotions (through devotionalism and virtuous behavior), the psychotherapeutic situation has, since the dawn of psychoanalysis, been characterized more by the expressions of *negative* feelings. Broadly speaking, while psychotherapy has been familiar with the value of the cathartic method, it has tended to disparage all attempts at an intentional cultivation of love; the roots of love and hate, in its opinion, can only be reached through delving into the unconscious. Conversely, spiritually oriented people usually are disdainful of expression of hostility, deeming it something that could only lead to the persistence of pain and the exaggeration of aggressive habits.

I think that it is more fruitful to consider both valid strategies—the traditional and the modern—not incompatible, but, rather, complementary: two therapeutic approaches that can be integrated. Catharsis does not in any way hinder the attempt to modify one's own behavior for the better; on the contrary, intentional virtue could very well lead to the repression of "nonvirtuous" emotionality if not complemented by the ventilation of present (nonideal) emotional life. As Alice Miller has reflected:[5]

> Religions say that we must forgive the injustice we suffered; only then will we be free to love and be purged of hatred. This is correct as far as it goes, but how do we find the path of the true forgiveness? Can we speak of forgiveness if we hardly know what was actually done to us and why? And that is the situation we all found ourselves in as children. We could not grasp why we were being humiliated, brushed aside, intimidated, laughed at, treated like an object, played with like a doll, or brutally beaten or both. What is more, we were not even allowed to be aware that all this was happening to us, for any mistreatment was held up to us as being necessary for our own good. Even the most clever child cannot see through such a lie if it comes from his beloved parents, who after all show him other loving sides as well. He has to believe that the way he is being treated is truly right and good for him and he will not hold it against his parents.

Just as too much spirituality without psychotherapeutic awareness can lead to the false goodness of a "deceptive spirituality" syndrome, too much grave-digging without a spiritual awareness may lead to a therapeutic impasse. Dwelling upon the pain of the past in the hope that more painful memories and more intense expressions of affect will bring about a liberation from the past may lead to disappointment, for such a liberation can only be brought about by the individual's willingness to apply what he or she has understood, by taking a stand in the face of the pain of childhood, obsolete behavior patterns, and the demands of the present. An orientation towards the cultivation of love and compassion, I think, is the specific factor that can end the situation in which the individual is a helpless consequence of the past.

The similarity between the Quadrinity Process and the psychoanalytic approach lies, most broadly speaking, in that both methods are predicated on the Socratic view that self-insight heals; they both recognize the importance of understanding our character and its origination during the early phases of life. Both set out to put an end to what psychoanalysis calls the repetition compulsion, the endless persistence of behaviors originated in childhood as a response to adaptation needs in one's family environment.

There are sharp differences between the two approaches, however, as to how they pursue this goal of liberation from emotional conditioning. Psychoanalysis discourages the patient's spontaneous tendency to analyze oneself in the course of treatment, appealing, rather, to the authority of the professional expert and regarding the individual's capacity for self-delusion as greater than the capacity for personal insight. The Process, on the other hand, capitalizes on the individual's drive for self-understanding. In assigning a considerable amount of biographic and self-exploratory writing, it not only recruits the individual's help but stimulates a greater continuity of attention, between sessions, to the psychological work at hand; for by spending part of each day writing, the individual remains in contact with the psychological situations that are being processed. A more important difference is that psychoanalytic technique relies on the therapeutic power of *destructuring* (mostly verbal) behaviors, and seeks to break up the individual's repetitive and compulsive patterns through free association, in which communication constraints that characterize usual nontherapeutic situations are broken. Hoffman's therapeutic method, on the other hand, consists of a mosaic of structured psychotherapeutic exercises and does not include free association. Directiveness is important in the structure. Hoffman's method is a *guided* process, in which an individual carries out specific instructions in regard to self-examination, written and spoken internal dialogues, visualizations, and so on. Most striking perhaps, the two approaches differ in regard to the simplicity/complexity dimension. "I found aspects which seemed to be those of a simplified psychoanalysis," says psychoanalyst Knoble, well aware that the simplified embodiment of psychoanalytic ideas did not come about as a result of any intention to simplify psychoanalysis. Also, in agreeing that the Process involves a simpler expression of analytic ideas than psychoanalysis, I don't want to imply a value judgement, for I would not criticize it for excessive simplicity more than I would criticize psychoanalysis for an excessive complexity. (A joke conveys the popular acknowledgement of this point: two psychoanalysts walking from opposite directions say "hello" as they pass one another on the street, and then stop, after three or four paces, to reflect, "What did he [she] *mean* by that?")

Psychoanalysis cultivates an awareness of the multiple determination of every mental and behavioral event. In the Quadrinity Process, a few simple and fundamental concepts are systematically applied in such a way that, in the span of only weeks, "psychotherapy virgins" emerge with clear and life-changing insights into their emotional conditioning, its childhood roots, and the desirability of taking distance from its compulsive way. ("One thing is to own a trait, another to be owned by it," says a caption on the wall of the Hoffman Institute.) One of these simple and fundamental concepts applied in the Process is what Freud called the repetition compulsion and in Hoffman's language is simply referred to as the "old programs"—a cybernetic analogy in line with the language of Perls and John Lilly. The main feature of these programs—for Hoffman as for Freud—is the dysfunctional adoption of dysfunctional parental behaviors and attitudes by the growing child through identification.

"In Freud's work," say Laplanche and Pontalis in their book, *The Language of Psychoanalysis*,[6] "the concept of identification comes little by little to have the central importance which makes it not simply one psychical mechanism among others but *the operation itself whereby the human subject is constituted*" (emphasis mine).

Whereas in psychoanalytic thinking a distinction is drawn between identification proper and introjection (in which the oral basis for identification is acknowledged by the individual), in Hoffman's view all neurotic identification is "oral" in nature and essentially introjective. The equivalent term for orality in Hoffman's vocabulary is "negative love," an expression suggesting not only destructive love but also inverse love, and implying false love as well. It makes reference to a seeking of love which stands in the way of love, wears the mask of love and is in fact opposite in nature to a loving motivation.

Whereas love is a disposition to give, born of abundance (to use Maslow's term), "negative love" is a wanting to receive, and is rooted in deficiency, though ordinarily experienced and presented to the world (while attached strings are hidden) as abundance and giving.

In his making "negative love" the central concept of an understanding of emotional sickness, Hoffman unwittingly echoes the view of Buddhism, which also interprets all suffering as having its roots in desire or craving (*tanha*). Expressions such as Maslow's "deficiency motivation" and Buddhism's "desire" or "attachment," however, fail to point out the connection of this deficiency to an early love frustration. And while psychoanalysis represents one step further in the direction of that acknowledgement, with its conception of orality, its excessive biologism (as contemporary psychoanalysts mostly agree) can be questioned.

And here we come to the most important theoretical discrepancy between Hoffman's view and the psychoanalytic: the fundamental frustration experienced by the child is seen by Hoffman as a *love* frustration rather than a *libidinal* frustration—oral or genital. While the sexualization of the love wish is common, Hoffman believes this to be a secondary phenomenon. (Even Kohut's reference to a child's "healthy narcissistic need" to be heard and seen ["mirrored"] by his mother seems to complicate unnecessarily the issue by failing to acknowledge the primacy of the love need that is expressed through such need for attention.)

Hoffman's idea that the child adopts parental traits in order to be loved somewhat echoes Freud's hypothesis in *Mourning and Melancholia* that we become like the lost person whom we love as a way of maintaining contact. Hoffman's interpretation not only acknowledges the love need as the basic source of identification, but implies an assumption in the child's mind that, by being like one's parents, one would obtain the love that one is not experiencing by merely being oneself. This psychological mechanism, sustained by "negative love," could well be called one of "seductive identification," and Hoffman claims that it may be found to be operating in most character traits.

Yet it is not only through identification that "the human subject is constituted," but through a superimposition of identification and counter-identification as well. Not only do we seductively adopt our parent's traits, but we rebelliously reject them, often at the same time, with the resulting conflicts.

The Process does not make use of dream analysis nor a contemplation of life between puberty and the present; yet it entails a sharper focus on personality development in childhood than is encountered in earlier therapies. Hoffman proposes that if deficiency motivated relationships to others are sustained by the persistence of a negative love relationship to our parents, it follows that this relationship with our parents must be healed. Only through self-love can the individual be in the position to love others, and only through restoring the original love bond toward one's parents can the individual in turn love himself or herself; for resentment against one's parents will unavoidably fall back upon the parental introjects permeating the person's psyche.

Healing the relationship between the individual and his or her parents does not come about through analytic activity alone, but requires (as in any successful insight theory) bringing into awareness the pain and anger associated with early life. The most healing kind of insight found along the path of self-understanding is, of course, beyond mere intellectual comprehension. It is inseparable from experiencing, which amounts to increased consciousness. And just as pain breeds unconsciousness, unconsciousness is perpetuated through the wish to avoid, deny, and repress pain.

With the advent of the humanistic movement, we have seen a shift in interest from the analytic to the expressive aspect of therapy; and the expression of pain, in particular, has been given a central role as a means of bringing into awareness the unacknowledged suffering of past and present. In Gestalt therapy, in particular, a quantum leap was taken from "talking about" experience to surrendering to it in an expressive disposition. Finally, the therapeutic potential of such catharsis was systematized and made the core of Janov's Primal Scream method. Hoffman also proposes a guided and systematic method for reexperiencing the pain of childhood. His particular contribution in this regard is systematization—brought into play through a blending of the analytical and cathartic ingredients. The history of pain in regard to mother, father, and parental surrogates is pursued in the Process through autobiographic writing and in the form of intrapersonal encounters between "father," "mother" and "child" components of the psyche. An aspect of the Process amounts to what could be called, because of the personification of a spiritual self along with the intellectual, the emotional, and the body-related sub-personalities, a "transpersonal psychodrama."

While the encounter between the intellectual and the emotional sides of the psyche, which Hoffman calls the "Adult Intellect" and "Negative Emotional Child," is somewhat equivalent to the Gestalt technique of under-dog/top-dog encounter, the body constitutes an original contribution. In Gestalt therapy, the awareness of the emotional core of physical experience is cultivated; in the Process, the body becomes a character in the internal psychodrama and is invited to express its experience of the individual's behavior and love in a way that elicits unique information.

Hoffman introduces a distinctive methodology to deal with the question: How can forgiveness be obtained?

> Genuine forgiveness does not deny anger but faces it head-on. If I can feel outrage of the injustice I have suffered, can recognize my persecution as such, and can acknowledge and hate my persecutor for what he or she has done, only then will the way of forgiveness be open to me. Only if the history of abuse in earliest childhood can be uncovered will the repressed anger, rage and hatred cease to be perpetuated. Instead they will be transformed into sorrow and pain at the fact that things had to be that way.

Forgiveness not only does not deny anger, it requires undoing the denial of anger that is part of the ordinary fallen and restricted condition of the psyche. And a valuable tool for the lifting of repression in regard to anger is, as in the case of pain, catharsis: for a close connection exists between the repression of feelings and the inhibition of their expression. In Gestalt therapy and encounter, compared to psychoanalytic therapy, a quantum leap has taken place in dealing with the expression of anger. The Process has brought systematization into the catharsis of aggression towards the parents as well: in powerful, experiential visualizations the Quadrinity psychodrama takes place among the adult intellect, the negative emotional child, the spiritual self and the body (in the presence of a spirit-mediating guide and in a spirit-imbibed, spirit-radiating inner sanctum), and provides the expression of anger together with the expression of pain. In addition, a technique called the "bitch session" is employed: a systematic expression of anger and condemnation towards the programmed emotional and intellectual aspects of the parents and parental surrogates in the early life history, focusing on the parents' personalities and particular events in the triadic mother-father-son/daughter relationship.

Is it true, however, that the "grace of forgiveness appears spontaneously when repressed [because forbidden] hatred no longer poisons the soul"? When hatred no longer poisons the soul, no doubt forgiveness can arise; yet I think that it is *hatred* that constitutes the poison, not *repressed* hatred. In other words, insight into one's hatred and giving oneself the freedom to express anger still may fall short of the transcendence of hatred. It is my impression that for some, the catharsis of pain and anger (provided by expressive therapies) is enough: the stimulus for further insight that pain and anger contribute is all that an individual seems to have needed to bring about a change of state. In other instances, however, one may see people "primaling" over extended periods and not truly moving forward, either in terms of insight or change. It would seem that, in these cases, a person's thirsting for a deepening of experience coupled to resistance leads to the replacement of insight by this pursuit of experience-intensification. As a relevant joke runs, "A Gestalt psychotherapist is a psychopath teaching obsessive compulsives how to become hysterics."

Alice Miller seems to imply that the grace of forgiveness does not always arrive in the course of psychoanalytic therapy: "The free expression of resentment against one's parents represents a great opportunity. It provides access to one's true self, reactivates numbed feelings, opens the way of mourning and—*with luck*—reconciliation" (emphasis mine).

I think that the great uniqueness of Hoffman's therapy is the systematic, directed, and assisted process that it offers for the transition from condemnation and resentment, through understanding, to forgiveness; so that forgiveness—the door to compassion, love, peace, and the deepest joy—may not remain a matter of luck anymore. And the strategy contained in the Quadrinity Process could be thought to be (by anyone ignorant of Hoffman's ignorance) a systematic application of Alice Miller's observations concerning those for whom forgiveness has dawned "as a form of grace" that "appears spontaneously" when "repressed hatred no longer poisons the soul." For after hatred has been transformed into sorrow, it will give way to understanding: *"the understanding of an adult who now has gained insight into his or her parent's childhood and finally . . . mature sympathy"* (emphasis mine).

The forgiveness-and-compassion process which follows each "bitch session" comprises a series of stages beginning for each parental figure in the individual's life with the reconstitution of the parental figure's life. Attention is particularly given to forming an image of our parents as they were in the process of growing up with their own parents. If it is understanding that can lead us to forgiveness, says Hoffman, it is a parent's early life in particular that we need to understand.

Intellectual and intuitive reconstitution is followed by a process of systematic empathy with our parents as they were when they were children, by means of identification through fantasized or dramatic enactment—common to Gestalt and psychodrama. This, in turn, is followed by a stage of the Process that could be called ceremony or ritual, as well as a guided contemplation. The type of intervention displayed here might be called behavior therapy at the attitudinal level through fantasy. What is involved is not the intention of changing behavior towards another at a later time, but doing so immediately, though in a guided and internalized psychodramatic situation. The therapeutic situation is now not that of looking into our experience or expressing it, but that of taking a stand, of bringing about an intentional modification of our disposition. I don't think the Process would be as effective as it is if it stopped at being an insight therapy enriched by expressive therapy methodology. An all-important component is persuasion toward a commitment to heed insight, to apply to life what has been understood, to responsibly take ourselves in hand. Work with fantasy may be regarded as a preparation for the post-therapy task of acting according to our understanding, and thus dropping those attitudes and behaviors that have been fully understood as obsolete and dysfunctional links in a chain that perpetuates suffering.

The activation of forgiveness and compassion toward the parents whenever they are alive provides sufficient motivation to support the most important task the Process assigns to the individual after therapy is completed: the taking of steps toward establishing a loving relationship with one's parents. Thus in the structure of the work, the forgiveness process constitutes a bridge between the individual's pre-therapeutic state of mind and the post-therapy practice it proposes: loving kindness in daily life. It is a bridge, too, between the analytic-expressive "personal" and the Judeo-Christian "transpersonal" sides of the Process.

The foregoing description of the Process makes it clear that we are dealing with an integrative approach. While psychoanalysis has remained faithful to the single technique of free association interpretation, the Process, while embodying essential insights of psychoanalysis, does not use the free association technique at all, but rather a composite of guided self-insight into early life history and personality, catharsis of pain and anger, and an attempt to inhibit the "ego" (in the sense of the spiritual traditions—the conditioned personality with which we have learned to identify). In addition, the Process comprises an important component of psychospiritual work through visualization and creative imagination.

A variety of techniques are employed in the Process belonging in the domain of work with visualization fantasy and imagery. However, the word "fantasy" currently used in connection with some of these may not be the most appropriate, for it fails to reflect the distinction between ordinary fantasy and the "high fantasy" of visionary experience. Hoffman refuses to call his guided trips fantasies, for, when these are deeply experienced, imagination only serves as a means of evoking another order of experience.

The invocation of a spiritual guide, for instance—instructions for which are given early in the Process—would be interpreted by a Jungian as an invitation to engage in dialogue with the "wise old man" or the "wise old woman" archetype within. Yet Hoffman, like shamans and other religious teachers, encourages his clients in an attitude of regarding the inner guide as an entity existing outside themselves (as distinct from the "spiritual self").

A New Tool for the Reeducation of Love

I think that many people today (generally speaking, the transpersonalists) believe that beyond the realm of fantasy there lies indeed a realm of experience which, when made conscious, is recognized by the ordinary mind as something that stands beyond it—an archetypal, visionary, psychic domain inhabited by the higher mind in the way that the ordinary mind inhabits the world of objects and logical classes. It would seem it is in this deepened state that the mind most displays the function referred to in its name, derived from the Sanskrit *manas*—related to both "man" and "moon." It may be that in the early linking of these two concepts, the human mind was regarded as a receptive moon facing the light of the spiritual sun.

Whether or not it is theoretically true that visionary and possession experience—including high inspiration—may involve something outside the individual psyche, I think it is *practically* true: it is an intellectual position that *brings about* the manifestation of the supraintellectual, protoarchetypal spiritual world of "creative imagination."

Thus no religion says, "Imagine God and talk to your imagination." On the contrary, by pointing to something beyond the individual self—a transcendent Thou, a Holy Other—many schools of traditional spirituality have demonstrated that it is possible to bring about the experience thus invoked. More generally, it may be said that the capacity to *absorb* oneself in symbols—thus entering contemplative states—goes hand in hand with an attitude of *not* regarding symbols as mere symbols, but rather, as that which they symbolize.

In virtue of the potential of symbols to stand in the place of the experiences that they symbolize (the basis of what Mme. Sechehaye called "symbolic realization"), certain imagery sequences can serve as vehicles for experiential shifts. Such "fantasies" might be regarded as rituals or ceremonies, and in the

Process this is the character of the all-important moment in the closing session when the client is directed to visualize umbilical cords connecting to the negative behavior trait-clusters previously examined in himself or herself and in his or her parents. The fantasy of pulling out these cords evokes the decision and will to separate from all the negativity that the previous analysis of the father and mother introjects has revealed. Like the forgiveness process, this constitutes a guided meditation, taking the individual through the attitudinal shift evoked by the symbolic action of pulling the umbilical cords and, using the symbol as a vehicle for reaching the deeper experience, imbuing the individual with the will to "ride" the vehicle.

A similar instance of the symbolic alchemy is that of "recycling," a visualization process that combines transpersonal and analytic components and which forms part of the individual's post-therapy assignment.

I used to feel that the individual who leaves the therapeutic process is unduly reinforced in the belief that he or she is completely healed. It seemed truer to regard the Process as a seed of something that may be fully attained in the course of a longer time, through a prolonged friction between the individual's conditioned personality and the newly adopted post-therapeutic intention. Indeed, today I regard the Quadrinity Process as an initiation into a different attitude, leading the individual onto a path of daily inner work, provided with motivation, the necessary outlook and psychotherapeutic tools to work upon oneself. Yet today my earlier criticism of the Process's claim to cure is tempered by the recognition that, in supporting an individual's sense of having been healed, at the appropriate time, the therapist introduces a most useful therapeutic technique: an invitation to relinquish the attitude of self-preoccupation that has characterized the therapeutic endeavor, thus adopting a position of abundance. The Process also constitutes an invitation to relinquish psychotherapeutic dependency and, above all, as Bob Hoffman puts it, to give up seeking to be, in order to simply be. In time, to be sure, whatever was swept under the rug will surface in the individual's awareness. Then the person will naturally grow more realistic about the full length of the "way of love" beyond the crossing of its first valley. But will that not take care of itself?

If one had wanted to create a synthesis integrating psychodynamic, transpersonal, humanistic, and behavioristic ingredients in individual psychotherapies, one could hardly have originated a better product that the short method outlined in this book. The Quadrinity Process fits into the historical pattern of the entire endeavor of psychotherapy *as if* it were a work of synthesis; however, it constitutes a gift of intuition, born away from the great world, so to speak, without reference to its apparent antecedents.

Just as in the sixties Gestalt therapy began to rival psychoanalysis in the United States, the Quadrinity Process has recently begun to rival Gestalt in some South American and European cities. Yet I believe that much of its potential benefit is still to be realized. I think, for instance, of its value for anybody wishing to become a psychotherapist. Yet I think most particularly of its potential in a future holistic education: that is, education that would reintegrate the affective and the spiritual aspects of human growth as its concern. The brief and definite time that this structured method requires makes it particularly suitable for groups in a school setting.

I hope that these words may further pave the way for the Process so that it can unfold its beneficial potential to individual mental health and also help nurture the development of such kindness as seems necessary for the success of our societal affairs.

Since I feel that I have been providentially alloted the launching of the Quadrinity Process into the world, it seems pertinent that I append to these reflections on the Quadrinity Process something about my personal involvement with the therapeutic and educational approach I am here recommending—for my close involvement with it has allowed me to be a witness of what value it has had for innumerable people, and it is this, in turn, that has implicitly supported my inclusion of this chapter in *The End of Patriarchy*.

I met Bob Hoffman at a private talk sponsored by Dr. Leo Zeff in Berkeley in 1972, in which he described the form of brief therapy he was practicing at the time. This was not a time in my life when I was seeking a new therapy. After years of seeking help from therapists and spiritual teachers I had come to what I call the "charismatic stage" in my life, when I felt, "I have gotten it" and was still excited about it. I do not think I would have registered for Bob's eight sessions of psychic therapy had it not been out of a generalized interest in the issue of inner father/mother/child relations in the transformative process—but it turned out to be a definitely valuable experience and I was impressed by the fact that Bob was able to describe for me my parent's life histories and events in my childhood that he could not possibly have known by ordinary means.

Also it seemed to me that the basic strategy in the Process through which he had guided me could be applied to groups, substituting Bob's psychic input with a structured, guided and supervised process of life recall and extrapolation from memories.

My first application was with a group of more than seventy people (culminating in Bob's visit for the closure stage of the Process). This was a time when, in my work with people at SAT Institute, I was particularly interested in the process of turning groups into self-healing systems. There followed a second application in which Reza Leah Landman led a group of about fifty people (with Bob present as silent witness) using

A New Tool for the Reeducation of Love

the format of written guidelines. (I produced these guidelines at a time of rare inspiration, and when I visited Bob shortly afterwords, he interestingly commented, quite spontaneously, that Dr. Fischer had been with me.)

The Process was appreciated enough in this and other SAT groups that many of my students became Bob's first collaborators, and so the hundred or so people that underwent the experience started an avalanche that began to spread.

When about a year later Bob conducted the first group of his own at the Berkeley Club, I was his guest, and I could see that our approaches differed: he sought to exclude the encounter and peer therapy elements; he perfected, instead, the delivery of feedback to his students' homework through tape recordings.

Since that time I have been a witness to the ongoing refinements in Bob's work and have continued to offer occasional demonstrations of my own version of it to groups in foreign countries that, little by little, have come in contact with Bob's organization in California. Brazil was one of the first countries in which it became popular. Today it is in the German-speaking countries that the Process is attracting the greatest interest.

It fell upon me, too, to be the catalyst for the more significant new development in the Quadrinity Process. When I described to Bob the great success that I had in Mexico working with a four-day condensation of the method, his eyes sparkled and he soon thought of developing his own "intensive" approach, which is now spreading forth in the world. The seven days that it lasts constitutes such a modest proposition in proportion to the results that I do not feel that another therapy may compete with it in doing so much within such a brief span of time. In spite of this, it is not the therapeutic potential of the Quadrinity Process that has moved me to speak about it in this book but, rather, its educational potential; for precisely the characteristic of being so brief and structured and yet so powerful makes it ideally suitable for inclusion in any educational venture that wants to address itself to the affective domain. Exposure to the approach would also be extremely useful for educators who are interested in acquiring a means of knowing better their students, themselves, and human beings in general.

"Within the safe enclosure of technical mastery, fountains of ancient mystery have once again erupted, peopling the landscape with familiar yet fantastic forms: gurus, shamans, wandering bards, exorcists. Against the bleak and secularized backdrop of our outer landscape comes, unbidden, a new cast of actors, costumed, beaded, and bearded, ready to act a play for which as yet we lack the script. Dancing they come, to an irresistible music, prying loose the gates of dream, unwilling to live without a myth."

STEPHEN LARSEN[1]

"What does it mean to take one's stand under the Dionysian, rather than the Freudian (or the Marxist) flag? It means to discard the pseudo-scientific posture of clinical detachment or political rationality, and recognize madness as the universal human condition, not the distinctive stigma of a separate class distinguished as insane. It means that madness is not an individual but a social phenomenon in which we all participate collectively: we are all in one and the same boat or body. It means also that madness is inherent in life and in order to live with it we must learn to love it. That is the point of honoring it with the name of a god."

NORMAN O. BROWN[2]

A NEW SHAMANISM FOR OLD ADAM'S PROBLEMS

1   The Problematique and the Kingdom

I began this book with a consideration of world problems (in Chapter I) then elaborated (in Chapters II and III) on some neglected solutions; it seems appropriate that I turn again to the problems as I draw to a close.

Looking at the *problematique* in Chapter I as a springboard to reflections on what I proposed as the root problem of civilization, I now turn to world problems as a prelude to the contention that, just as the root of our problems is intimately human, so is also the cure we must seek, and our main resource.

The proposition to the effect that the patriarchal structure of the mind and society constitutes our number one problem is not to be found, that I am aware of, in the many discussions of world problems in the United Nations organizations. Similarly, I do not think that the resource I am about to discuss and propose as critical has been explicitly taken into account among the many specialized books dealing with the problematique. Yet it is the corollary of an old teaching, to the effect that everything takes care of itself if we only mind "the Kingdom of God."

The explicit thesis of the chapter, then, is that human transformation continues to be neglected in current approaches to the problematique, and that our main resource in the face of the crisis that we navigate is the subpopulation of individuals in transformation—a world of seekers who struggle with themselves and that I here discuss under the rubric of "new shamans."

2 World Problems

U. Thant, Secretary-General of the United Nations, said on the occasion of United Nations Day in 1970 that, "It is unforgivable that so many problems from the past are still with us, absorbing vast energies and resources desperately needed for nobler purposes," and after reviewing such problems as the armaments race, racism, violations of human rights, and "dreams of power and domination instead of fraternal coexistence," he observed that "while these antiquated concepts and attitudes persist, the rapid pace of change around us breeds new problems which cry for the world's collective attention and care: the increasing discrepancy between rich and poor nations; the scientific and technological gap; the population explosion; the deterioration of the environment; the urban proliferation; the drug problem; the alienation of youth; the excessive consumption of resources by insatiable societies and institutions. The very survival of a civilized and humane society seems to be at stake."

All this is today widely known. What is perhaps not so well known is that—as U. Thant proceeded to remark—"the seriousness of our situation derives not only from the mere multiplicity and gravity of problems and awaiting solutions but from the fact that between these multiple problems there exists an incalculable number of interrelationships which, whether ascertained or not, greatly restrict the range of action open to the policymaker."

The more we understand how the solution of each isolated problem may constitute in itself a problem in view of other problem situations, the more it seems that we need to focus on root troubles rather than on particulars.

The limitations of an approach to problem-solving that remains exclusively practical and symptom-focused is vividly brought to mind by a 1973 report by the United Nations Secretary-General: "Acute problems, when they arise, may emerge in the form of commercial, financial or monetary imbalances that appear to be localized in particular countries or groups of countries. Deeper analysis will, however, often show that the problems of one country or group of countries in one sphere are intimately related to concomitant problems in other countries and in other spheres and that adequate overall solutions depend on parallel and consistent measures in several different fields, having regard to the interests of all countries. What may appear to be a problem unique to one sphere may be symptomatic of wider and more far-reaching tensions in the international economic system as a whole."[3]

Because of the many interrelationships between problems and the interacting of problems there arises the hydra-like phenomenon in the problematique. Just as the mythological hydra renewed its heads after they were severed, so our problems are bound to renew themselves every time we attempt to do away with them without regard to their interrelationship, for "there is, then, no such thing, in isolation, as the population crisis, the urbanization crisis, the pollution crisis, the armaments crisis, the oil crisis, the energy crisis, the fertilizer crisis, the resources crisis, the water crisis, the soil crisis, the fish crisis, the technology crisis or the trade crisis. Each of these crises acts on the others, and while it may be useful to focus attention on them one at a time, none of them can be solved unless the others are taken into account."[4]

The very fact that due to the complexity of the mutually interacting problem system "no combinations of purely technical, economic or legal measures and devices can bring substantial improvement"[5] to our situation calls not only for interdisciplinary approaches, as The Club of Rome has observed. I think that, most importantly, we need to take heed of the notion that our problems are not only man-created but that they are the consequence of an evolutionary arrest (i.e., the neglect of psychospiritual growth at the individual level.

To point in the direction of inner growth, healing and enlightenment may sound anti-economic, but is it dispensable?

"While the difficulties and dangers of problems tend to increase at a geometric rate, the knowledge and manpower qualified to deal with those problems tend to increase at an arithmetical rate," says Yehezkel Dror in his prolegomenon to policy sciences,[6] while Cellarius and Platt remark, "Many important steps are now being taken to meet these problems. These steps, however, are often shaped to fit existing institutional patterns or to be politically or commercially expedient, while other measures of perhaps equal or greater importance have not yet been started. Moreover, the multitude of crises and their complexity and interactions so overburden the mechanisms that have been designed to handle them that there is a valid fear that these mechanisms will break down at the critical moment and make the disasters worse."[7]

Kahn and Wiener say, ". . . the world is becoming so complex and changing so rapidly and dangerously and the need for anticipating problems is so great, that we may be tempted to sacrifice (or may not be able to afford) democratic political processes."[8]

The hopelessness of the piecemeal approach is all the more apparent when taking into account the absence of consensus of specialists concerning priorities. I read in the 1984 *Encyclopedia of World Problems* that "in 1974 Jan Tinbergen noted that only two years after the (Pearson) report of the International Commission of Development suggested accelerated growth for the developing world, the results of The Club of Rome study indicated the necessity for decelerating world growth."

Our main hope lies in the fact that the most serious problems facing humankind result not only from the direction of social, economic, political but from *psychological* forces. The extent to which this is so is quite evident from an analytic consideration of the very list of world problems.

The authors of the 1984 *Encyclopedia of World Problems* (Yearbook) have carried out the laudable task of indexing (from data in published documents—mostly from international organizations) over 8,000 world problems ranging from earthquakes and diseases to economic domination by multinational corporations and lack of coordination between international organizations. In addition to indexing and cross-referencing this long list, they classified its entries into nine categories according to the following code (from "A" to "F"):

1. General to specific: classes of phenomena, such as living species, are allocated "b" at the kingdom level (e.g., plants) down to "g" for a specific species (e.g., bald eagle), or a specific disease or commodity.

2. Universality: all classes ("a") of living beings, for example, through to particular classes or specific types ("e"), such as tropical islanders.

3. Fundamental to dependent: ("a" through "e").

4. Hierarchies: top of several hierarchies ("a") to a specific feature of a single hierarchy ("e" or "g").

5. Discipline: transcending any group of disciplines ("a"), through major conjunction of disciplines ("b") to single discipline ("d") and subdiscipline ("e").

6. Geographical/cultural locus: From global ("a"), without any specified region or division, through intercontinental ("c"), such as developing, industrialized or socialist, to specific ("d"), such as mountain or tropical regions, through multiple qualifiers ("e") such as "disabled women in developing countries," to problems of one single country which are of wider significance ("g"), such as apartheid.

7. Set membership: where the problem name suggests the possibility that the problem is a member of a set of similar problems, they are coded "c" or lower. For example, "blindness in children" suggests "blindness in the elderly."

8. Fashionable problems: care has been taken not to give exaggerated prominence to highly publicized specific problems (e.g., endangered species of whales, AIDS).

9. Exceptions: The code "f" has been used for potential problems, dormant problems, extraterrestrial problems and various subtle or intangible problems.

According to this convention, then, 105 problems were assigned to the "A" group—the category corresponding to the more general, universal, fundamental, transdisciplinary and intercontinental.

It is most revealing, I think, to find that 38 among these 105 are distinctly psychological problems, while 27 are both outer and inner problems, such as abuse of power and domination. I list the psychological ones here: abandonment, absurdity, aggression, alienation, angst, anxiety, apathy, arrogance, avarice, boredom, complacency, cruelty, dangerous substances, deceit, dehumanization, depersonalization, egoism, elitism, evil, fatigue, fear, fragmentation of human personality, frustration, humiliation, incompetence, indifference, insecurity, loneliness, malevolence, negative emotions attitude, obsession, pride, psychological inertia, spiritual void, superstition, vanity, vice, violence.

It has been the message of this book thus far that we can only expect to overcome our problems by regarding ourselves as the number one problem. It is in this particular chapter that I develop the notion that (symmetrically) it is in ourselves—not only individually but collectively—that the solution lies.

An old English saying advises us to "take care of the pounds and the pennies will take care of themselves." If the pounds in the subject of our discussion is what the prophets of old called the Kingdom of God, it is remarkable how little it is taken into account in the most sophisticated discussions of specialists. Let us consider, for instance, the report of the Director-General of UNESCO at the 18th General Conference (Paris, 1974) concerning the analysis of problems and table of objectives to be used as a basis for medium-term planning (1977–1982). The major world problems identified as such were as follows:

> 1. Human rights; 2. Peace; 3. The advance of knowledge—scientific and artistic creativity; 4. Exchange of information; 5. Communication between persons and between peoples; 6. Concepts and methodologies of development; 7. Policies and strategies for development; 8. Infrastructures and training for development; 9. Greater participation by certain groups in development; 10. Man's natural environment and its resources; 11. Man in his environment; 12. Population.

Rewording the statement we may say that the problems of injustice, war, ecology and overpopulation require, in the view of UNESCO, more exchange of information, communication, concepts of methodologies, policies, infrastructures, trainings, etc. To the notorious left-brain bias of such a proposal, I feel like responding as I did to Alexander King's list of educational objectives. It would seem to be implied that knowledge is equated with wisdom, and that love is implicitly regarded irrelevant. As for the transformation of the individual into a compassionate being, the fact that it does not enter into the discussion may be taken as the expression of a feeling that this is something about which nothing can be done. As a further response I proceed to the following discussion of new shamanism and the proposition that, as life only proceeds from life, the cultural rebirth on which our future depends can only arise from healed and spiritually ripened individuals.

3   New Shamanism

I think that among the ideas that I have generated throughout my life, that of a "neo-shamanism" may well be the one that has found the greatest popular resonance, and in view of this I feel less original today as I set out to discuss the subject than when I coined the expression. All the same, I think, the discussion belongs here—inasmuch as we have not altogether transcended, as a culture, the arrogant and xenophobic attitude through which we have practically stamped autochthonous shamanism out of existence and particularly because of a peculiar relevance of the shamanic spirit to the healing of patriarchal consciousness.

Suspecting that this might be the last time when I undertake the interpretation of our recent cultural movement, I feel moved to approach the matter in a way that retraces the gradual unfolding of my thinking on the subject.

I don't know when exactly I began to think about this, but I do remember clearly that the idea was in my mind by the middle of the sixties, when I came to Berkeley from Chile for the first time. There was something shamanistic about the place and the time. I had the good luck of crossing paths with Carlos Castaneda, and even became the person closest to him before he had any thought of writing books. This, aside from my work and ideas, may have inspired someone to describe me in an Esalen catalogue as a shaman.

By then I read with great interest Eliade's book on shamanism (which appeared in Spanish before it did in English and, I think, continues to be the most important contribution on this subject).[9] My respect for Eliade's work was enough to insure that I would not make the mistake of believing myself to be a shaman, in the full sense of the word, but being called one did make me aware of something "shamanistic" in my inclinations and in my style. Also, my self-awareness brought me to realize that the designation of "shaman" was losely applicable to other people I knew.

I was fully aware of the issue as I wrote *The One Quest*[10] in 1969. As I contemplated various approaches to human development in view of their potential applicability to education, it became clear to me that three broad realms of culture and society needed to be considered: that of health and medicine, that of education and development, and that of religion with its goals of salvation and enlightenment. These three endeavors could be seen to typically converge in our time, and they constituted a single domain in the remote past—when in the figure of the shaman were superimposed the roles of spiritual guide, healer, and initiator of the youth into the mysteries of the culture.

We are living in an age of synthesis in which the crumbling down of artificial barriers among domains of knowledge and schools of thought is making possible new information bridges. Though the process of synthesis is continuous in the course of cultural evolution, a more intense integrative process began to manifest in the scientific realm some decades ago with the emergence of interdisciplinary concerns and a transdisciplinary approach. Also in the spiritual domain we have become more ecumenical to the extent that the breaking down of authoritarianism and dogmatism (which authoritarianism brings along with it) allows us to understand the natural unity of things. The convergence of the spiritual concern, the therapeutic, and the educational that was embodied in the rise of the "Growth Centers" during the sixties and seventies seemed to me a manifestation of a rediscovery of the intrinsic unity of concerns underlying our artificial compartmentalizations.

Yet in insinuating in *The One Quest* that the strivings for salvation, healing and maturation converge in our consciousness and point to a unity that was explicit in the days of shamanism, I had not come to the point of articulating the expression "new shamanism." I would do so later, at the 1977 Annual Conference of the Association of Humanistic Psychology which took place in Berkeley, under the title of "Common Ground."

My address at that conference served as an opportunity to introduce an esteemed compatriot who had recently arrived in California and whose work could hardly be described more appropriately than that of a modern-day shaman. I gave my talk the title "New Age Shamanism," which I then proceeded to use interchangeably with "neo-shamanism" as I spoke of the convergence between the therapeutic and the spiritual, and also of other convergences that in our time evoke the way in which a shaman is homo-religious, artist, and healer. I proposed that shamanism has to do essentially with a synthesizing attitude, and that it characteristically involves a synthesis of reason and intuition.

We can think of civilization as having always alternated between times in which reason has dominated, and times in which emotions and intuition are valued and expressed preferentially: classical times and romantic times. The influence of Rousseau, for instance—father of Romanticism—contributed significantly to the unleashing of the French Revolution. Yet once the revolution triumphed, it was the goddess of Reason that became enthroned. Romanticism made its appearance again, later, and our recent "human potential movement" could well be considered a new romanticism.

Yet I would say that in the decade of the 1960s, the pendulum reached its maximum excursion in the direction of intuition and disdain of reason, and now it is returning. Now we find ourselves at a time of special opportunity toward a new synthesis. Not only is the intellectual sphere valued again, but we glimpse the importance of a meta-synthesis that could encompass the analytic activity of reason and the synthesizing activity of intuition.

A notable case of such convergence between the synthetic and the analytic aspects of the mind is to be found in the intellectual movement of modern physics with its awareness of parallels between the old intuitions of mystics and the new formulations of quantum physics, for instance. Already, before the most recent development of physics, in the days of de Broglie and James Jeans, this convergence between reason and intuition was clear enough within physics so that Bogumil Jasinowski, teaching History of Culture at the University of Chile (and of whom I had the privilege of being a student) could say that he regarded the modern physics as a reemergence of Neo-Pythagorean thought. It seemed to him that for the first time in history, it was possible to find this convergence of attitudes and interests that have mostly diverged in the days since Pythagoras—the love of mathematics, reason and science, on the one hand; and a mystical orientation, on the other. After the famous "Copenhagen interpretation" of quantum mechanics, in particular, it may be said (using again an expression of Jasinowski) that physics has ceased to be "organoleptic," for what it describes cannot be visualized; it escapes every kind of map that we may draw.

Much earlier than the convergence between the science and mysticism in the minds of the early Pythagoreans, we can discern the same situation in the case of shamans, who were the first scientists, investigators of nature, and first experts on fauna and flora, cultural ancestors of the earliest ironsmiths; for these proto-scientists were also the earliest mystics.

But beyond saying that among the old shamans and (increasingly) among the new, we are finding two-brained beings—that is to say, people with a greater balance than what has been common to find between the left, rational, analytic hemisphere, and the right, intuitive, synthetic brain—we can also say that the old and the new shamans stand out as being *three*-brained—for the process of personal integration is not only a matter of a convergence between right and left brain. It may be said that as our rational brain ceases to exercise absolute monopoly over our neuropsychic system, not only is the intuitive brain liberated, but also all that which Professor Rof Carballo called, some decades ago, the "inner brain"—intimately linked to the emotional world. And this is not all, for if we are to speak of an integration between the cognitive realms (rational and intuitive) and the emotional, we cannot neglect to bear in mind that the old shamans have been before all else people who have reconnected with the most archaic layer of their psyche—that which is sometimes symbolized through animal spirits and particularly through the snake—that remote ancestor of ours that we all carry within the most primitive part of our brain and even in our day continues to be emblematic of medicine.

If it were not that the old shamans and their contemporary heirs are endowed with a greater emotional health than average, they truly would not have their characteristic capacity to heal. Nor would the shamans be artists without the basis of an intense and free emotional life. Today much of the task of therapy consists in becoming aware of emotional life and liberating an individual's capacity to experience and express his or her own emotions. Those who assist others in this task cannot do it "by the book," without having gone through their own intensely personal process of anguish, awakening, and liberation.

According to Dr. Paul MacLean, we are three-brained beings in that we are endowed with a cerebral cortex (which constitutes a particularly human part of our human nervous system), an emotional brain that we share with mammals, and an instinctual brain that we share with reptiles. To the extent that this is so, ancient shamans were simply the first people who lived to fulfill the potential totality to which we all aspire, consciously or unconsciously.

One of the most remarkable characteristics in the history of civilization has been its turning against instinct—an opposition that Freud and later Toynbee considered an insurmountable tragedy. Koestler, in collaboration with Toynbee, claimed that a *discontinuity* has arisen between our instinctual brain (inherited from our reptilian ancestors) and the more recent development in our nervous system that constitutes the basis of thinking and of our attempt to rationally control our life: a discontinuity amounting to a loss of the instinctual capacities of a sane animal. Yet both in old shamanism and in the new shamanism that is emerging before us, we have an indication that this discontinuity is functional and not irreversible; thus the "animal within" may be reintegrated into the conscious psyche and it may be possible to reach a condition of complete, truly three-brained beings.

True as it may be that through rational control we have lost the instinctual capacity of a healthy animal and that there is a discontinuity between the instinctual and rational spheres, we need not share Koestler's pessimism inasmuch as it is not necessary to conceive this discontinuity as immutable biological fact. It is enough to conceive it as a chronic imbalance perpetuated throughout the evolution of society and culture. Indeed, the reintegration of the instinctual to the sphere of the conscious psyche has been, explicitly or not, a task modern psychotherapy has been tackling with increasing efficiency. Psychotherapy began with Freud who, like Koestler, was a pessimist in regard to the possibility of integrating instinct and civilization.[11] With the passing of time, however, the simple restoration of awareness (through the reintegration of the repressed) came to be coupled increasingly with an orientation toward the liberation of impulses—and thus there arose a faith in the intrinsic innocence of humans. Wilhelm Reich and D. H. Lawrence were pioneers of this point of view now generalized in humanistic psychology.

An interest in the hallucinogens that link shamanism with contemporary culture and innovative psychotherapy (in spite of orthodoxies and governmental control) reveals a high measure of confidence in the deep spontaneity of the psyche, both on the part of those interested in undergoing such experiences and on the part of those who have assisted them. However true it may be that medical and other authorities have been mostly concerned with the additive potential of these substances in our society (for little has been done by way of providing a channel for their considerable healing potential), I believe that historians may have occasion to appreciate how they have contributed to the breakdown of the patriarchal social ego in recent decades. We cannot ignore the inspiration that they brought to the pioneers of the counterculture, which has, in turn, lent decisive inspiration to our recent cultural development. It is noteworthy, too, how the upsurge of interest in the therapeutic and spiritual endeavor was stimulated through the contributions of those who (like Aldous Huxley, Hermann Hesse, and Ram Dass) were assisted toward another level of health or awareness through pharmacologically induced experiences some decades ago.

It is not accidental that the new culture and the new therapies have become interested, as old shamans were, in hallucinogens. It is not only a matter of recovering the deep spontaneity of alienated instinct. I think that an important aspect of eclectic, humanistic, existential psychotherapy has been what might well be called *faith* in what Gestalt therapy calls "organismic self-regulation."

A theme that is intimately related to that of the arousing of the instinctual is that of the liberation of a spontaneous healing and evolutionary process for which we may well continue to employ the old Indian word *kundalini,* for I understand the so-called "kundalini" as no other than the awakening of our reptilian brain which, in turn, I envision as much more than an instinctual-homeostatic apparatus in relation to physical sustenance: I envision it also as a psychic "organ" of self-regulation at subtler levels of the psyche, a guiding function along the individual evolutionary path. The kundalini process, so characteristic of shamanism and of tantrism, has found an upsurge in our time in which certain psychotic or physical experiences are being reinterpreted as "kundalini accidents," and specialized centers for their attention have arisen.*

Even though tantric texts speak of kundalini as a power which, in the form of a spiral, lies at the base of the trunk and may rise through the axis of the body to the crown of the head, resulting in the fullness of the experience of the divine, there has been much mythologizing about kundalini, and also considerable mystification. Without falling into the pitfall of literalism, however, we may say that the activation of kundalini encompasses various levels, each of which is intimately related to shamanism: the physical level (through the prana and opening of the chakras), the emotional level (ecstasy), the mental level (visionary capacity), and the spiritual level proper—with its marks of sacrality and transcendence.

Among the different aspects of kundalini it may be useful to concentrate on one which is particularly characteristic of shamanism. When Gopi Krishna[12] speaks of it as an "evolutionary force," he means to say that kundalini is much more than a source of spiritual motivation. The kundalini energy involves a *guiding* principle, so that the process of personal development *from there on* becomes rather autonomous and spontaneous. While in each spiritual tradition there is a recognition of an inner condition by which the person feels guided by higher forces or beings (a Sufi, for instance, is sometimes defined as one who is guided in this manner from within), it may be said that the shaman is, *above all else,* guided by his or her inner guide/guides. In shamanism there is only a minimum of instruction in the sense of transmission of codified knowledge.

---

*The American SEN (Spiritual Emergency Network) founded by the Grofs has occupied itself much with this subject, and recently has been responsible for the organization of the first international conference centered on the kundalini process. There also exists in San Francisco a kundalini clinic.

Characteristically, the ways of shamanizing are always quite individual, for shamans display a high degree of uniqueness in their way of guiding others.

I have heard a Hassidic tale about a rabbi who was asked about the sources of his knowledge. He answered, "Everything I know I have learned from my father; he didn't imitate anybody and I don't either." Likewise the shaman. Along with a subtle spiritual contagion, the shaman inherits an example of freedom and originality in his (or her) approach to the higher world and way of serving the community. Each shaman has his own power objects, his own tales to tell, and above all his own inspiration; the same may be said of the new shamans—who (unlike therapists of competing schools in past decades) are becoming not only more eclectic but more personal in their style and in the contents of their "bag of tricks."

If the statement on the part of traditional shamans to the effect that they have learned from spirits was once received with benevolent disbelief by voyagers and anthropologists, today the phenomenon of inspiration has received a popular validation comparable to that of simple intuition and visionary phenomena. A testimony of this is the dramatic rise of interest in parapsychology. Also, I think it is relevant to mention that while only a few poets in modern times speak to us of their inspiration as a voice that has resounded in their ears, in the world of psychotherapy at least one of the existing and successful methods of today originated in such a type of inspiration, comparable to a shamanic revelation: the Quadrinity Process, of which I have spoken at length, did not arise from reflection or from trial and error, but distinctly (at least to the mind of its originator) as a psychic communication.

The wide recognition that inner or higher guidance currently is receiving is also manifest in a proliferation of clairvoyant advisers and therapists who regard themselves as shamanically guided in their work.* Also "channelling" has become prominent in contemporary American culture as a whole. This term makes reference to what happens to people who offer themselves receptively to messages beyond their conscious mind, as in the case of automatic writing and the process behind the writing of books such as *Seth Speaks* and *A Course in Miracles*.**

The phenomenon is old. But the veritable explosion of channelling indicates a generalized public interest and reveals a disposition on the part of many to open up trustingly to what lies beyond the limits of their personality. We may say that channelling is an aspect of the psychic and shamanic *zeitgeist* of our day.

In his benchmark study of shamanism, Eliade begins by discussing shamanic vocation—and justly so, for the shaman's calling is a dramatic event and is the first stage of shamanic experience proper. A shaman is typically someone who is *called* in a rather exact sense (that is to say, in the deepest and somewhat forgotten sense of the word "vocation")—and this calling has taken the form of acute sickness. Jung has spoken of a "wounded healer" archetype, but however much this image abounds in mythology and folklore, the original reference of the symbol is to the actual reality of shamanic vocation as we know it throughout time and in all cultures.

Whereas medicine and psychology are transmitted—as other professions are in our culture—by a passing on of infor-

---

*As I revise this chapter an issue of the *Journal of American Academy of Psychotherapists* ("Voices: the art and science of psychotherapy," volume 28, number 4, Winter 1992) has just appeared that is devoted to the subject ("Psychotherapist and Shaman").

**A thick, self-help manual received by an experimental psychologist with no previous beliefs in the beyond or in what came to constitute the unfolding contents of the book.

mation and practical training, in the phenomenon of vocation there is (aside from individual predisposition) the influence of a factor of contagion. The same may be said to be true in the Freudian explosion and, more generally, in the present explosion of neo-shamanism. When I was a student at the University of Chile Medical School there still did not exist a School of Psychology in my country. Now there are more psychology students than law students, while law school was the most attended in earlier years. In the whole world, the proportion of people attracted by psychology has increased impressively. A specific enterprise has embodied the spirit of each of the epochs that have followed upon one another throughout the story of our culture. Just as in the nineteenth century it was biology that dominated and influenced the culture most, and just as in the days of Galileo it was physics, we may say that our recent "human potential movement" has not been so much the result of progress in any of the professions or academic circles, but an expression of this collective turn of the mind that has manifested in the therapeutic domain, in the spiritual and, more specifically, in an increasingly spiritualized psychology.

Because of the contagion factor, I think that the new shamanism, to the development of which we are assisting, has exploded beyond the limit of any profession, and this has originated some debate at the edge of the professions. It was the medical doctors who for some time had the monopoly of psychotherapy; then it was permitted for psychologists to practice it too, and still later the privilege was extended to social workers; yet now the explosion has gone beyond, and many are turning into amateur psychotherapists while professionals have appealed to the law in order to seek custody of their privileged territory. In Spanish we have the expression "we all have something of the doctor, the poet, and the madman." This is more or less like saying we all have something of the shaman.

For the shaman is one whose capacities are the natural consequence of a contact with his or her deeper being. We can say that the deeper being of all is "shamanic."

The sickness that makes the shaman (whether it comes to him as an outer accident or as a plunging into an inner abyss) is not the only form of descent into hell. Just as the usual development of the kundalini process is that of an ascending movement of body energy through the chakras that is followed by a descent, in the unfolding of consciousness that parallels such physical changes, a period of expansion of consciousness is followed by one of contraction. Correspondingly we know of shamans who make their journey to the heavens before their journey down to the underworld. It is because of this that kundalini has been considered dangerous: for one insufficiently prepared or insufficiently guided not only is kundalini the gateway to ecstasy—it can also be a doorway to agony (as is dramatically illustrated by Gopi Krishna's autobiographic account). It is part of a path of inner purification and to a greater or lesser extent, an inner dying process—a disintegration of the obsolete personality or conditioning that the individual developed during the earlier part of life.

During the expansive phase of the shamanic process and even during the ascent of the kundalini we may speak of a psychotic aspect, in a broad sense of the word: a "higher psychosis," a mystical madness inseparable from the path, necessary to know as such in order to transcend. Cervante's *Don Quixote* constitutes, basically, a contemplation of this condition of an insanity that is a path. While writers such as Cervantes and Goethe have understood that a higher madness is part of the illuminative path (and already in the Middle Ages there was a widespread recognition of a sacredness in madness), we can generally say that our culture has been very far from offering psychotics the understanding, acceptance and companionship that is appropriate. This is, to say the least, very different from the acceptance and expert guidance which shamanic cultures knew how to offer those who entered the path through sickness, permitting them a mental voyage through the world of madness and a processing of this madness until the point when the individual emerges from it not only wiser, but with an ability to heal others.

Only in the new psychological movement is it possible to find a substantial change in the view of psychosis. Since R. D. Laing in particular, psychosis has been conceived by some not just as something which medicine has the obligation of curing, but, rather, as a "positive disintegration" (to use Dabrowski's expression), or a regression in the service of a progression, a descent into hell that can effect a purification. In our culture, where statistical "normality" is far from true psychological health, the conception of psychosis as a path rather than an accident along the way continues to be revolutionary, even some twenty years after the Esalen Institute invited Laing to the United States and brought together the reunion of a number of specialists who, in the course of a month or so, reflected on "The Value of Psychotic Experience."

Modern tolerance of madness seems to be a corollary of a more generalized tolerance of altered states of consciousness, a new openness before experience and a capacity of surrender that suggest the appropriateness of the expression "dionysian" to define the new spirit. Already toward the end of the past century Nietzsche prognosticated "the gradual reappearance of the dionysian in our contemporary world," and it may be said that particularly the cultural revolution of the 1960s has been of a "dionysian" nature. This was observed by the theologian Sam Keen in the eulogy of the emerging psychospiritual revolution contained in a book that he called *To a Dancing God*.[13] In this, too, our new spirituality echoes shamanism, since the spirit of Western Christianity, like that of the "other religions" in general, is Apollonian, whereas traditional shamanism is dionysian.

The idea that the spirit of our time is shamanic and dionysian may serve as a background to an understanding of other manifestations of it, ranging from the interest in hallucinogens (a form of "drunkenness" in the dionysian sense of "letting go") to a familiarization (through the therapeutic process) with that madness which, as Melanie Klein proposes, underlies the strictly neurotic layer of our mind.

Beyond being a god of drunkenness and surrender to impulse (to the point of madness) Dionysus is a god who dies and is reborn—or, rather, a god in whom surrender to madness and the transformative process of death and rebirth become a single process.

The subject of death and rebirth is the central issue in the Christian religion, and is one that is present, in one or another form, in every spiritual tradition, whether this is stated in a symbolic mythical way or through abstract concepts—as is the case of notions of *Faná* and *Baqá* in Sufism or those of *Nirvana* and *Enlightenment* in Buddhism. Yet we may say that in the high religions the codifications of experience and the conceptual teachings formulated around them distract us from the experience itself, and it is thus that those anthropologists who were the pioneers in the attempt to understand shamanism (notably Rasmundsen among the Eskimos) had occasion to be surprised that experiences that we attribute to the historical Christ or other avatars were described in a rather regular way by the "primitive" subjects of their interviews.

For a shaman is, perhaps beyond anything else that I have indicated until now, one who has died and who has been reborn: one who has firsthand experience in the transformative process, intrinsic aspects of which are a psychological death and a spiritual birth. Yet what can be described from one point of view as an ascent to Heaven and a descent into hell is, from another point of view, a journey into the beyond that, as in Dante's allegory, involves at first leaving the world behind and then being reborn into it. Beyond the experiences of ascent and descent, the shaman is, as Eliade emphasizes, most characteristically, a "lord of the three worlds": one who has acquired the capacity to *visit* heavens and hells without dwelling any longer in them; one who has access to ecstatic and other experiences and yet has developed detachment toward the spiritual as well as the mundane. To use an archaic shamanistic metaphor, he or she can move upward or downward along the world axis, coming to rest in the middle region—which may be of interest to bear in mind in our days of neo-shamanism, since it signals the critical difference between a shaman and a sorcerer's apprentice.

Also of this facet of the shamanic process—its being a process of dying and of being reborn—it may be said that it has reemerged in our dionysian times. Among many things that could be said concerning this, let me cite in the first place the recent interest in near-death experiences (which American researchers generally designate with the abbreviation NDE).

Just as many shamans began their way without seeking it, through the proximity of death (possibly through an encounter with a fierce animal or a serious illness, for example), many individuals today are reporting transformative experiences precipitated through automobile accidents or surgical deaths, among others. Maslow discovered decades ago that peak experiences were not so unusual as it was believed, and many could report one or more of them in the course of their life; now it is being discovered that near-death experiences are not so scarce either, and many people have been not only affected by them but launched into a process of inner transformation.

Another instance of a modern interest in death could well be called that of the "new thanatology"—the renewed interest in helping others who are near approaching their own death through specialized support, as in respect to its acceptance and spiritual guidance, such as in the pioneering work of Elizabeth Kubler-Ross and the initiative of Ram Dass and his collaborators. It is significant too, in connection with this subject, that *The Tibetan Book of the Dead* has become a pocket book in the U.S. This surely reflects not only a re-actualization of the idea that the living may help the dead, but a certain understanding that the message of this book can be valid in connection with a process of inner dying and rebirth in life. E. J. Gold's book *The American Book of the Dead* is worth a mention in this connection because it explicitly emphasizes, through its description of "bardos," the validity of such observations for *this* life, and particularly the validity of the traditional instruction of holding on to one's center without succumbing to fear or attachment in situations of pain and turmoil.

Something similar may be said concerning rebirth: even though the concept of the second birth is fundamental to Christian doctrine, there are many more people (with or without a religious background) who feel they have come to a new beginning in their life than was the case in the time of our parents and grandparents. Intensified change entails an intensification of inner dying that is part of our normal life, inasmuch as we unlearn and leave things behind; it also entails an intensification of an inner birthing that is always present in our openness to the moment. Today there is more clarity, in general, in connection with this process of psychological death and the birth of a spiritual awareness. Psychedelic experiences and the systematic attempts at suspension of the ego through meditative practice have made many familiar with the process, and also specific techniques such as Rebirthing and Holotropic Therapy have inspired some recognition to the effect that "as above, so below": as in the biological realm, so also in the psychospiritual.

The psychological experiences of death and birth that are elicited by hallucinogens have contributed to the reactivation of the old subject. Of particular significance have been the reflections of Dr. Grof who has put forward the idea of a parallel between the biological stages of birth and the psychological realm through his notion of "perinatal matrices." Already Freud had suggested that the so-called "oceanic" experiences known to mysticism might constitute an echo of intrauterine life. For Grof, nevertheless, this is not all: the hellish experiences of the adult, characterized by a sense of eternal condemnation and despair would be an echo of that primal pain that may be assumed that the fetus undergoes when the contractions have started in the womb but dilation of the cervix has not yet begun. According to Grof, this was a time when we felt incarcerated, closed-in and oppressed or suffocated. On the other hand, the death-like experiences of the adult would involve an echo of that which we all probably underwent when, as we emerged from the intrauterine world, we felt that approached the end of our existence.

Some ten years ago (under the auspices of the Goethe Institute in Chile) I had occasion to speak concerning "integrative psychology and new shamanism." I then preferred to speak of "integrative psychology" in view of being before an audience not too familiar with "transpersonal psychology," and in the U.S. today it would have been normal to speak of *"transpersonal* psychology and new shamanism"—for transpersonal psychology has not only defined itself as holistic, but the interests of those identified with it make it the most characteristic academic crystallization of the new shamanic spirit of our time.

As I then presented the notion of a close association between our new shamanic *zeitgeist* and the eclectic, synthesizing and nondogmatic spirit of contemporary psychology, I intended to develop more than I previously had the idea that the newly developing forms of "bodywork," which Dr. Thomas

Hanna has called "the new somatologies," are also embodiments of our new shamanism. For those who in the recent decades have trained themselves in the different schools of bodywork that have emerged since the school of Elsa Gindler and the breathing therapies in Germany at the beginning of this century, or in the approach developed by Mathias Alexander in Australia, as well as Rolfers, bioenergetic therapists and others, move in a nonverbal realm that requires a rare combination of intuition and body awareness. Also, among the experts of these different ways of approaching the mind through the body, there is the recognition of the typically shamanic experience of body-energies, itself the manifestation of what I have already discussed as the kundalini phenomenon. Particularly striking is the specific instance of Wilhelm Reich, whom we can even consider a rediscoverer of the kundalini in our times.

As I set out to speak of the shamanic spirit of the human potential movement on this occasion, however, I found myself rediscovering that in the same way that the recent revolution in consciousness has constituted a new blossoming of the Freudian revolution (from which it became differentiated, but on the shoulders of which, so to say, it found support), so, too, the new shamanism of which I was speaking was nothing more than a flourishing of an earlier shamanism *inseparable from the origins of modern psychotherapy.* For the greatest contributors in the early development of psychotherapy bore some of the most characteristic traits of the shaman. Sigmund Freud, to whom we owe more than anyone else our present psychological orientation, is a case in point.

I have often said that Freud, more than a scientist, was a writer, and that it was appropriate that he was awarded the Nobel Prize in *literature.* He could also be called a prophet, even though he did not believe in a better world, but only pointed out our ills. I suspect that the time will come when we will be able to say about Freud (as of Marx) that much of what he thought was obsolete, and then it will be obvious that his true contribution was not that of his scientism but his prophetic stature—embodied in the impulse that his search for self-knowledge effectively injected into our culture.

We may regard Freud a cultural hero who had the great courage of recognizing and illuminating his own neurosis—without being necessarily more neurotic than his "average normal compatriots" (perhaps even somewhat healthier than most). His courage to look into the abysmal—as shamans do—was to constitute a seed of a generalized recognition of the malaise and the emotional disease in post-Freudian times.

As is well known, Freud fell unconscious on the day of his father's funeral, when he recognized that, as his patients, he too had hated his father—whom throughout his life he thought he had loved so much. When in an act of so much honesty to himself he discovered his "oedipal hate," the ferment arose of what would become, with the passing of time, the notion of the universal neurosis of mankind. For if Freud's mind was not substantially different from that of his patients, didn't this imply that most of us share this same vicissitude? It was only a matter of time for the idea of the universal neurosis to become credible in the world.

I think that an important link towards this generalized understanding and acceptance was the analysis of the psychology of capitalistic society undertaken by Erich Fromm. It must be remembered how, after he wrote *Escape from Freedom*[14]—in which he had undertaken the analysis of the Nazi phenomenon—Fromm argued in the *The Sane Society*[15] that modern American capitalism was not necessarily healthier, but only pathological in a less visible way. He claimed that the irrationality that stands out when we contemplate our collective life panoramically constitutes an amplification of a pathology that is so pervasive (socially patterned) that it has become invisible to us at the individual level.

The awareness of a social pathology and of the near-universality of individual pathology, negligible at the time of Freud, has developed with the passing of the years, along with a progress of psychological awareness in general. Perhaps the most eloquent analyst of a crazy world has been R. D. Laing, in whom the absurdly catastrophic condition of ordinary human relations is almost implicit, while he concentrates on showing us the extent to which what is called "love" is often secret violence, and that the way in which apparently healthy and well-intentioned individuals treat children (who consequently become schizophrenic), once deeply and attentively considered, is not what it seems to be.

I think that through this awareness of a pathology of the culture on the whole—once pioneered by Freud—some of the most awakened among us have become somewhat marginal much as the shaman in the past was (conscious of the shared madness of humans) somebody transcending his own culture: one who, leaving the world behind, attained a condition of such striking value to others that the community reinvited him as a guide.

But let me continue with the theme of a shamanistic quality to our "psychotherapeutic lineage." I use the term "lineage" in a broad sense to suggest that, whatever the distance may be between the level awareness of our new-Freudian therapists today and that of the great masters of the East in connection with whom the term is mostly used, there has also been among us a line of transmission that has involved a contagion—one usually mediated by the therapeutic process and which goes beyond professional education proper.

If we attentively consider the case, we see that the tree that Freud planted was not truly a tree planted by Freud, for Freud became interested in psychotherapy as a result of a specific interest in hypnosis; and hypnosis, in turn, was introduced in

Europe by another "modern shaman"—a person as extraordinary as today forgotten: Mesmer, who first put into practice in European society the healing trance. Psychologically less sophisticated than Milton Erikson has been in our times, we may yet consider him not only one of the new shamans (for essentially he was an intuitive, and his work rested on the use of altered states of consciousness) but one more shamanic in his activity than even Erikson was, for the emphasis of his work lay in an appeal to the healing potential of the organism. For something basic in his activity was an implicit invitation that he extended to his patients: to let go of their nineteenth century's "social identity" and allow the deeper wisdom of their psyche to operate freely on their pending problems.

After Mesmer, there followed an explosion of interest in hypnosis, and Freud, after his visit to Charcot, began to work with the induction of trance. Alas, he became frightened when a patient once impulsively kissed him in the presence of his housekeeper, and from that day on he replaced hypnosis with an ingenious method that, in course of time, developed into the technique of free association. If in terms of cultural history it was Mesmer who planted the tree of psychotherapy, then, Freud watered it and grafted it.

Another figure of great influence in the history of psychotherapy, and more particularly in the humanistic movement (ambivalently new-Freudian and counter-Freudian) was Wilhelm Reich. One of his merits was that of going beyond the orthodox vision of repression as an inevitable perturbation of consciousness—a result of an incompatibility between civilization and instinct. Like Norman O. Brown, Herbert Marcuse,[16] and others who came later, Reich believed in a liberation of *impulses*, and particularly in the liberation of sexuality. Like Freud, Reich contributed beyond psychology to culture in general through his antiauthoritarian attitude and his promotion of sexual freedom. He was a new shaman in regard to a different aspect of shamanism than those considered in relation to Mesmer and Freud: the psychotic experience proper.

Some Reich enthusiasts have sought to negate or minimize his madness—but this is not necessary. He is an example of a certain kind of person in whom madness and genius coincide, and his psychotic traits should not invalidate his best ideas. On the contrary, it would seem that psychosis is sometimes the result of a personal incapacity to confront too much truth, becoming a kind of price that the individual pays for an openness of perception that others would not tolerate. In some cases however, deep perceptions are combined in a mixture of truth and distortion—as is typically the case in that schizophrenic symptom called "literal interpretation of metaphor."

Reich's messianic grandiosity not only led him to demand a recognition from the scientific world for thoughts that were beyond the realm of his expertise, but he interpreted the lack of such recognition (particularly in the absence of a response from Einstein in regard to a letter on his ideas concerning time) as proof of a government plot. He believed that he was observed by planes which crossed the skies over his home, and his son Peter describes (in a small autobiographic book) how his father ordered him to bury his watch so that it would not poison the environment with the anti-orgonic energy of its phosphorescent numbers.

Shamans, as we know, undergo a psychotic phase and manage to heal in the context of a culture that offers them help along the way. We do not know whether Reich could have been healed after his prosecution and federal imprisonment, but we may surmise that it is more difficult to heal in a complex and shamanically impoverished culture.

Carl Jung, the pioneer of today's transpersonal orientation of psychotherapy and a spiritual heir of Freud (much beyond what the ideological differences between them would allow one to think), also illustrates shamanic characteristics. They are somewhat hidden as a consequence of his circumspection and a somewhat "Swiss" personality. Though visited by spontaneous parapsychological events and interested in the most fascinating spiritual subjects, he appeared before his contemporaries as somebody relatively conventional, and even his rather revolutionary gesture within psychoanalysis may be deemed as somewhat *counter*-revolutionary. Yet it is also true that his rather controlled way of presenting himself to the world served to disguise an exalted aspect that was as present in his life as it was in that of other pioneers of psychotherapy. Those who know more of his private life through his journal, for instance, know of his personal familiarity with the psychotic domain, and can appreciate that one of his most brilliant contributions to psychology—the concept of inflation—originated in firsthand experience. He shared with Freud, then, a keen awareness of his disturbance and I am sure that—also as in Freud—his permeability to his unconscious was the key to his vocation and healing capacity.

Even more of a shaman than any of those whom I have discussed until now, however, through his way of practicing psychotherapy (perhaps as a consequence of having lived at a later time and in a culture more congruent with the shamanic spirit), was Fritz Perls.

I had the good luck of being able to be near Fritz before he became truly famous. He was relatively unknown yet, at the beginning of his life in California. I worked at the Institute of Personality Assessment and Research on the Berkeley campus of the University of California, and one day I received the unusual invitation of Dr. Michael Harner, who worked at a short distance on the same campus and whom I had known some months earlier. Michael Harner, then director of the Museum of Anthropology at the University, was at the moment with Carlos Castaneda who, in turn, was undergoing the beginnings of his shamanic apprenticeship. He proposed that the three of us offer a joint workshop in "an interesting little place by the ocean about four hours at the South of San Francisco"—a little-known place called Esalen, which was to become the prototype of hundreds of Growth Centers throughout the world in the years following.

Fritz was not working at Esalen, only had settled there because he felt it was the best place to live, and in view of this we found ourselves in the interesting situation of having him among the audience during our work. As is well known, Fritz was not an easy person in any sense. Not only did he practice that advice that was so characteristic of his, of chewing well before swallowing (and swallowing only what is assimilable) even more, he seemed to spit out more than he swallowed. Thus he reacted with a combination of disdain and arrogant competitiveness to the presentation of Elsie Perish, a Pomo Indian shamaness (also invited by Dr. Harner) who spoke of her dreams and other early manifestations of her vocation. Before a small group of us, in the course of the intermission, Fritz said what amounted to "if she is a shaman I am too," for it seemed to him the most natural thing to act in accordance to the inspiration of visions. He gave an example: "some days ago I was with a woman who talked and talked and I didn't know what to say or do. I closed my eyes and I saw a barking dog. I understood and said 'you sound to me like a barking dog.' She began to cry and said, 'my husband tells me the same thing.' Everything got moving in the therapy from then on."

Fritz's disclosure impressed me. I had known him through his writing but never imagined him as a person. I felt great admiration for his capacity to be open to images that for most people remain as subliminal, or only emerge under the intensified gaze of therapeutic or spiritual explorations. This contributed to my eventually coming to train with him. Fritz was not only a shaman in the sense of working with images and intuition, but was also a spiritual person (a crypto-taoist, I would say) in spite of an antireligious posture, and his activity resembled very much that of some shamans who act as experiential guides moment after moment. Moreover, he combined spirituality and animality (he once described himself as fifty percent son of God and fifty percent son of a bitch) in a way characteristic of shamans, who are never sanctimonious and whose benevolence is not moralistic.

Although nowadays we are witnessing a generalized interest in shamanism, the most usual idea is that to become a shaman means to look beyond our culture and learn from Eskimos, from Navajos, from Australians, and so forth. All this is very well. There is wisdom in traditional shamanism, and I am personally pleased with the thought that the dying shamanism of old cultures may be transmitted before the modern world erases them. Also, it will be salutary to our own overcivilized culture to encounter people who never fell into its own aberrations.

However, this mushrooming interest in ethnic shamanism prompts me to point out what is autochthonous in our emerging Western shamanism and to emphasize that it is possible to recognize a lineage of our own, a line of shamanic continuity that is ripening in the course of time.

Many have adopted the idea of a new-shamanism among us—perhaps because their form of spirituality is more dionysian than that of classical religions, perhaps because by calling themselves shamans they feel empowered in their activity. Many, surely, feel narcissistically stimulated in viewing themselves in the elevated and mysterious role of shaman—and even that can be inspiring, not only for them but for others. I only want to suggest that we don't forget the distance between a sorcerer's apprentice and a true sorcerer. A shaman is not just one who has known altered states of consciousness or who embraces a magical view of the world, but one who has come to ripeness through a deep transformation.

Precisely in the midst of present enthusiasm regarding shamanism, it may be of interest to understand shamanism as a transcultural phenomenon: something that has not so much to do with any particular tradition, but rather, has existed in every time and in every culture without necessarily being called "shamanism."

Let me give two illustrations in regard to this transcultural conception of shamanism. One, the observation during my research in the sixties, on the effects of the drink known as *ayahuasca*[17] that is used by some South American shamans as part of their training. A striking finding, then, was the recognition with which my subjects—uninformed as to the origins of the experimental substance—had visions of jungle cats, snakes and birds of prey. While anthropology has thus far considered ayahuasca visions as something socially transmitted—the result of the cultural influence over the individual who partakes of the "jungle brew"—my experiences with volunteers in Chile at the time allowed one to conclude that such experiences (typical, by the way, of shamanism beyond the Amazon) could be understood as *not* culturally conditioned, but as something latent in every human being.

The next example will be appropriate at this point, for it refers to an artist, and I have thus far concentrated on shaman-like therapists. Also, it allows me to evoke, toward the end of this book, the person with an account of whose thinking I began.

While I do not doubt that when the vast poetic work of Totila Albert becomes known it will find its place among the classics, it is not anything in his work that I want to discuss now, but the experience that precipitated his entry into the path—an experience of spontaneous initiation that, in his own words, marked the end of his first life and the beginning of a second.

About a decade after the event, he described the experience in a poem entitled "Winged Body" in which his deceased parents ask, "you rise in flight, son?" and he answers, "Holy voices, I think yes" and proceeds to remember how his soul mourned them and how all he had was "the shadow of emptiness" until pain opened his body.

> Thrust the inside out,
> and with the force of sound
> there sprouted wings from the abyss.

Body sensations and visual hallucinations seemed to combine here in the feeling that his body split in halves along the spine and that what was inside became wings. We may say that the experience was at the same time uniquely individual—as the bas-relief with which he sought to express it and I have used to convey the dialectics of father-mother-child; yet the themes of body opening and inside-out turning, together with that of flying and the transmutation of the hellish into the heavenly (wings sprouting from the abyss) are shamanic. Most shamanic, however, was the sense of turning into a great bird of prey (an experience sculpturally rendered through the condor that holds the son in his claws).

Today we know through writers such as Eliade about the Siberian shamans who regard themselves—in view of their characteristic inner initiation at the beginning of their shamanic life—descendents of an eagle-like primordial shaman. But I am sure Totila knew next to nothing about shamanism, and nothing about Siberian shamans; his shamanism was not borrowed, but intrinsic, and his interpretation of his experience was not suggested by a cultural model. Yet like Siberian shamans he entered—from this time onward—a visionary world; and the experience was deeply healing (inasmuch as it entailed a coming together of his "inner three"). To say that the eagle or the condor are archetypes doesn't explain anything; it only describes the fact that certain experiences (and the symbols through which their physical and mental aspects may be evoked) are not necessarily the echo of a culture, but may be considered intrinsic to the unfolding of human experience—built-in regularities along our potential path. (I am convinced that the sensation of being rent apart along the axis of his body was an expression of that eminently shamanic phenomenon to which I have referred with the traditional Indian word *kundalini*, though this was neither part of the vocabulary of shamans nor of his.)

I hope that through such examples I may have made it clear that when I speak of a new shamanism I am no longer speaking of the same thing as those who believe it to be something strictly linked to drums, feathers and totem animals. The shamanism developing among us certainly bears connection with ethnic influences, but we should recognize that an autochthonous shamanism emerged even before today's generalized awareness of primitive mysticism and healing—and only because of an affinity between the emerging shamanism and the archaic have we become interested in the latter.

I think that especially in our times—when so many sorcerer's apprentices undergo what I have called the "post-illuminative inflation syndrome," or the deep regression involved in a later stage of incubation—it is meaningful to lend attention to the idea that no matter how half-baked the present generation of new shamans may be, we may expect them to play an important role in the collective transformation which we are undergoing. In this population of somewhat marginalized seekers then, may lie a sort of "crazy wisdom" and human

The Bird of Returning, Totila Albert

resource of greatest significance for our critical predicament. For certainly our effective response to the crisis will not come from the old institutions, but from a new ferment.

If it is true that, as I have been claiming, the transformation of the world presupposes individual transformation and that the critical resource in the explosion of individual transformation is the catalytic influence of individuals who are transformed or on their way to transformation, then the practical corollary is clear. The wise and the seekers of wisdom have always existed, but what is new in our days is the possibility to take our situation in hand, collectively becoming agents of our development through fostering inner change and through intervention in the economics of the situation. It is easy to envision new large-scale and supervised self-help ventures: consciousness-raising groups for the poor (a ripening analog of the politically oriented consciousness-raising groups of the past); scholarships for nonintellectual and yet deeply educational ventures; and the employment of local shamans along with the new psychospiritual methodology.

As I draw to a close, I feel moved to bring in a metaphor known since antiquity in connection with individual transformation: the butterfly; only that in offering it as a symbol of collective transformation I envision a sort of macro-butterfly, each cell of which is an individual who (through inner pilgrimage and incubation) had left behind his or her original larval condition.

I once heard Willis Harman say that the metamorphosis of the butterfly involves, during its incubation in the chrysalis, not only the disintegration of old cellular structures, but the emergence of a central structure formed of cells which, because of their control on the formation of the future organism (of which it may be said to contain a blueprint), have been called "imaginal cells." Just as the imaginal cells of the butterfly precede the transformation of the larval body into the adult winged body, we may envision the pioneers of individual transformation of today as "imaginal cells" coming to constitute a transformative element as our larval (patriarchal) society undergoes metamorphosis into a Kingdom of Three.

POSTLUDE

It may seem strange that an economist should be the one to write the postlude to this book. I have enough reasons and intuitions for doing so. Nevertheless, the audacity is Claudio Naranjo's for having asked me to write it.

It so happens that as the years go by, especially *my* years, which have already taken me to the latter stages of middle age, to the extent that I have gradually lost certainty I have become aware of certain things, the figuring out of which, in the form of an intellectual project, partly justifies what is left of my life. My concern focuses on three enigmas, and for the elucidation of the three of them I have found stimulating contributions in the essays which make up this book: a) our defective capacity to understand, b) the incoherence of our language, and c) the reification of the need for freedom.

As beings who use complex language, we know how to describe and, frequently, how to explain phenomenons, events, processes. It is by such language games that we have accumulated and put in order the totality of our knowledge. On the way, brutally accelerated since the scientific revolution (Bacon, Descartes, Galileo, Newton), we have perpetuated an error which today is becoming, in my opinion, obvious. We have assumed that describing plus explaining equals understanding. But, in fact, *understanding* is a different matter. Describing and explaining has to do with knowledge (with the learning) corresponding to the realm of science. Understanding, however, rather emanates from experiences of enlightenment which correspond to the realm of wisdom.

To illustrate the difference between *knowing* and *understanding*, imagine a person who has studied all there is to study—from a theological, anthropological, psychological and even biochemical perspective—about a human phenomenon known by the name of love. The result is a person who knows everything about love, but will never *understand* love unless he or she falls in love. By withdrawing from our object of observation or study we can acquire knowledge about it; but we can only try to understand that with which we integrate, that of which we become a part.

In the field of learning—as is pointed out in the essay Claudio writes about education—we look on the world as the sum of many problems. We detect them and design solutions for them. In the field of understanding, on the other hand, it is not a question of detecting problems, but rather of being and making oneself a part of transformation. The attitude of "I have nothing to do with the environment," "I have nothing to do with nature," "I have nothing to do with social problems," eventually turns us into experts who, by accumulating solutions, perpetuate the problems. Thus, we experience and face a paradigmatic metamorphosis, that is, a profound transformation like the one affecting our world today, as if it were only the vast sum of many problems. The conclusion arising from this observation is perhaps the actual essence of the mega-crisis

Postlude

we are experiencing; the reality of having reached a state in our evolution in which *we have a great deal of knowledge but understand very little*. This would not be a cause for concern if it were not for the fact that the great challenges which humanity now faces require nothing less than that they be understood rather than merely known.

However, why do the things that happen take place? What we know, we know because it can be expressed through language. What we are able to know is, therefore, outlined by the limits of language. What we understand, on the other hand, lies beyond the limits of language, because it refers to the profound attributes of things which, as such, can neither be described nor explained, even though they can be apprehended. Let us imagine a trivial example: a number of manuscripts by various persons with different handwriting. In all of them the letter "a" obviously appears in many and varied ways. Some leaning toward the left and others toward the right, some long and others short, some thick and others fine, and so each has its own style, with a tail and even without one. When we read the texts we always recognize these letters as "a"; because what they all have in common is the profound attribute of their "a-ness." We perceive that "a-ness" holistically; that is to say, we understand it, but we cannot describe it nor explain it. Wittgenstein has already said this: "About that which we cannot speak we must keep silent." Here lies our permanent error: we try to force everything to fit into language.

If what we know can stimulate a discourse, what we understand can only be translated into an attitude. For this reason—and also because of what Wittgenstein pointed out—"there cannot be ethical *principles*, there are only ethical *attitudes*." Both trivial "a-ness," and transcendental ethics are profound attributes, of things or of somethings, which go beyond the limits of language and belong, therefore, to the realm of silence.

Knowing and understanding. Language and silence. The most beautiful aspect of language is, without a doubt, its capacity for giving meaning to silence. Thus, a step toward the reconstruction of our own selves as beings who are not only fragmented but also capable of being complete, as Claudio Naranjo calls for, aims at learning the wonderful role of "balancer" of language and silence, the only occupation allowing us to render to knowledge what belongs to knowledge and to render to understanding what belongs to understanding.

But even where language is useful, we have frequently used it wrongly. "Each generation has its issue," said Ortega y Gasset; and we may add that each generation is also educated by some language. A good part of the Middle Ages was dominated by a language with an underlying theological preoccupation; that is to say, of justification for the ultimate causes. This gave rise, among other manifestations, to monastic life, the great cathedrals, poverty as a way of life, knight-errantry and the Crusades. The nineteenth century is the century of the nation-state, as its dominant language reveals when we read the great treatises of Disraeli, Gladstone, and Bismarck. Our century is the one that falls under the spell of artificial, economic language as the bearer of images of progress, growth, development and modernity.

There is nothing wrong with being educated by a language, as long as that language is coherent with the challenges which the generation in question must face. Let us see, to this effect, what has occurred in the last seventy years. Between the end of the twenties and the beginning of the thirties, an era known as the great world crisis, the language of Keynesian economics emerged. This language is the product of a crisis, but has the potential to interpret and overcome this crisis. It thus is a question of a language which is coherent with its historical challenge. The next change comes about in the fifties, with the emergence of the language of development. This language, contrary to the previous one, is not the product of a crisis, but rather of the optimism resulting from the spectacular economic reconstruction of postwar Europe. It is an optimistic language with the underlying supposition that the recipe for eradicating poverty in the world has finally been found. The magnitude of the changes and transformations characterizing the fifties and the sixties is sufficient so as to also attribute to that language a certain coherence with the contemporaneous historical challenges. After this come the seventies and the eighties, characterized by the emergence of the enormous paradigmatical crisis which is our current concern. And then the unusual occurs. The new period, so new that comparable historic precedents cannot be found, does not originate a new language. Quite the contrary, a language sustained by unlimited enthusiasm for growth and economic expansion in the face of an increasingly conspicuous reality of social, political, environmental and ecological collapse prevails with more strength than ever. We are dealing with a situation of *incoherence between language and historical challenge*. This is the other cause for concern in the mega-crisis which it falls to us to experience.

All language is the product of a culture, as well as the generator of culture. Furthermore, the way in which we use words and concepts influences both our behavior and our perceptions. Hence the danger of a "catechetical," economically oriented language such as the one currently prevailing over a great part of humanity.

Let us examine three premises of the "catechism" mentioned above: a) consumption will make me free; b) in order to be free it is not enough to be a person, one must be a consumer; c) the more I consume, the freer I am. Once these premises have been accepted (and it is astonishing to see the number of people in our present world who do accept them), the awaited miracle occurs for the believers: the market attains an ontological justification! In effect, the market is the only uterus capable of giving birth to consumers! Everything is consummated: freedom does not lie within the *being* but rather in the *having*. My language has molded my world. My world is my language. But since my world is not the world, because the world is what it is, salvation is still possible, and Claudio suggests paths.

What and how much does what I have set forth above have to do with the essays making up this book? I think that the answer lies in the first of these essays, the one which has moved me the most. Not only did it reveal to me an unknown dimension of Totila Albert, whom I knew in my childhood, but it also allowed me to find, through the thinking of this tragic sculptor, particularly in his idea of "that which is thrice ours" (the patriarchal, the matriarchal and the filial as an inseparable trinity), anchorage for the reflections which I have delivered here. Let us see.

Totila Albert says, through Claudio: *"The paternal, maternal and filial principles are independent of sex and age.* The function of the paternal principle is that of fertilizing, producing, giving form to the gift of life from bread to art; the function of the maternal principle is receiving, nourishing, educating, and giving up the complete being to life; the filial functions are development, learning, desiring and being free." Our work consists mainly of making the balance of power between the sexes equal, as well as that between the components, and feminine domination of the "amazonian" type, focusing on patriarchal values, would be of no use to us whatsoever.

I have the feeling that the paternal lies in knowledge and language, the maternal is revealed in understanding, and the filial is expressed in the design of freedom. Thus, my three enigmas find refuge in Totila Albert's lucid "thrice ours." Should this convergence be legitimate, my initial reflections would reveal a world in which the paternal has become incoherent, the maternal has become discredited, and the filial has been objectified. Such a situation would completely justify

Postlude

Claudio's urging that we must "accelerate our transition from the patriarchal hierarchy of our mind toward a heterarchical, tri-centered organization of father, mother, and child."

The project has been proposed. Nevertheless, an evident danger prevails. How do we construct a heterarchy from within the hierarchy? How do we liberate our actions from a language that dominates our surroundings? Perhaps we need to design a meta-incoherence in order to overcome the incoherence tying us down?

We do not know how to do what we have to do, and that is good. We do not have certainty, and that helps. We need to discover, and those who know exactly where they are going are precisely those who never discover anything. Once who knows exactly where to go has only two obsessions: the point of departure and the point of arrival. All the space that lies in between is perceived as an obstacle to be overcome as soon as possible and with the greatest possible efficiency. It so happens, however, that the entire adventure of life, that all the possibility of discovery, lies exactly within that space which we discard as a nuisance. Paraphrasing our old deceased politician: "Certainty engenders nothing, only uncertainty is fertile." But uncertainty alone is of no use. One must know how to work on it.

The only useful substitute for those who are prepared to renounce certainty is *learning to drift in a state of alert*. Instead of having a clear picture of things, prick up the antennas of perception. In order to find the new answers we must again become accustomed to asking questions.

For drifting in a fertile way and asking relevant questions, Claudio's essays are a feast for the explorers of a world that is waiting to be discovered.

> Manfred Max-Neef, Executive Director of the
> Alternative Development Center (Chile), Member
> of the Executive Council of The Club of Rome,
> Alternative Nobel Prize in Economy (1983)

NOTES

Foreword / On and For Our Times
1. *Shambala/The Sacred Path of the Warrior,* by Chögyam Trungpa, Shambala, Boulder, CO, 1984.
2. *The Triune Brain in Evolution,* by Paul D. MacLean, Plenum Press, New York, 1990.
3. *A Study of History,* by Arnold J. Toynbee, Oxford University Press, London, 1935, 1961.
4. *The One Quest,* by Claudio Naranjo, Viking Press, New York, 1972.
5. *No One is to Blame: Getting a Loving Divorce from Mom & Dad,* by Robert Hoffman, Science and Behavior Books, Inc., Palo Alto, CA, 1979.
6. *The Turning Point: Science, Society and the Rising Culture,* by Fritjof Capra, Simon & Schuster, New York, 1982.

Chapter I / The Agony of the Patriarchal Order
1. *The Creation of the Patriarchy,* by Gerda Lerner, Oxford University Press, London, 1986.

2. *Apocalypse And/Or Metmamorphosis*, by Norman O. Brown, University of California Press, Berkeley, CA, 1991.
3. Capra, op. cit.
4. Naranjo, op. cit.
5. *The Decline of the West*, by Oswald Spengler, Modern Library, New York, 1965.
6. *The Making of a Counter Culture; Reflections on the Technocratic Society and its Youthful Opposition*, by Theodore Roszak, Doubleday, Garden City, NY, 1969.
7. *The Limits to Growth*, by Donella H. Meadows, et al., Universe Books, New York, 1972.
8. *The Year 2000*, by Herman Kahn and Anthony J. Wiener, Macmillan, New York, 1967.
9. *The Electronic Sweatshop: How Computers are Transforming the Office of the Future into the Factory of the Past*, by Barbara Garson, Simon & Schuster, New York, 1988.
10. *An Incomplete Guide to the Future*, by Willis Harman, San Francisco Book Co. Inc., San Francisco, CA, 1976.
11. Capra, op. cit.
12. *Myth, Religion, and Mother Right: Selected Writings*, by Johann Jakob Bachofen, Princeton/Bolligen Paperback, 1973 (original German publication, 1926). Bolingen Series LXXXIV, Princeton University, Princeton, NJ.
13. *The Mothers*, by Robert Briffault, abridged with introduction by Gordon Rattray Taylor, George Allen & Unwin, Ltd., London, 1927, 1959.
14. *The Language of the Goddess*, by Marija Giambutas, Harper & Row, New York, 1989.
15. *Patriarchal Attitudes*, by Eva Figes, Fawcett Premier Book, Fawcett World Library, New York, 1971.
16. *Gyn/Ecology: The Metaethics of Radical Feminism*, by Mary Daly, Beacon Press, Boston, MA, 1978/1990.
17. *Le Feminisme ou la Mort*, by Françoise d'Eubonne (in Mary Daly, p. 9).
18. *The Chalice and the Blade: Our History, Our Future*, by Riane T. Eisler, Harper & Row, San Francisco, CA, 1987.

19. *Up From Eden: A Transpersonal View of Human Evolution,* by Ken Wilber, first edition, Anchor Press/Doubleday, Garden City, NY, 1981.
20. *The Masks of God: Oriental Mythology,* by Joseph Campbell, Viking Press, New York, 1962.
21. *Retroprogressive Essays,* by Salvador Paniker, Editorial Kairos, 1987.
22. *The Great Cosmic Mother: Rediscovering the Religion of the Earth,* by Monica Sjoo & Barbara Mor, Harper & Row, San Francisco, CA, 1987.
23. Paniker, op. cit.
24. *The Mismeasure of Woman: Why Women are Not the Better Sex, the Inferior Sex, or the Opposite Sex,* by Carol Tavris, Touchstone Books (Simon & Schuster), New York, 1993.
25. *You Just Don't Understand: Women & Men in Conversation,* by Deborah Tannen, Ph.D, Ballantine, New York, 1990.
26. *Androcles and the Lion: An Old Fable Renovated,* by Bernard Shaw, Penguin Books, Baltimore, MD, 1957.
27. *The Meeting of the East and West: An Inquiry Concerning World Understanding,* by F. S. C. Northrop, Collier Books, New York, 1974 (1946).
28. *Global Mind Change,* by Willis Harman, Knowledge Systems, Inc., Indianapolis, IN, 1988.
29. *Leisure, The Basis of Culture,* by Joseph Pieper (Alexander Dru's translation), New American Library, New York, 1963.
30. *The Great Turning,* by Craig Schindler and Gary Lapid, Bear & Company Publishing, Santa Fe, NM, 1989.

Chapter II / Educating the Whole Person for the Whole World

1. *La Primera Revolución Mundial,* by Alexander King and Bertrand Schneider, Plaza and Janes Editores, S.A., Barcelona, Spain, 1991.
2. H. G. Wells in *Toward a Psychology of Sustainability,* by Roger Walsh, Revision Journal, Fall 1991.
3. *New Rules: Searching for Self-Fulfillment in a World Turned Upside Down,* by Daniel Yankelovich, Random House, New York, 1981.
4. *No Limits to Learning: Bridging the Human Gap,* by James W. Botkin, Mahdi Elmandjra & Mircca Maletza, Pergamon Press, New York, 1979.

5. "On the Education of an Amphibian," in *Tomorrow, Tomorrow, and Tomorrow, and other essays*, by Aldous Huxley, Harper, New York, 1956.
6. *Anatomy of Thinking*, by Abercrombie.
7. *Thinking for Yourself: Developing Critical Thinking Skills Through Writing*, by Marlys Mayfield, Wadsworth Publishing Company, Belmont, CA, 1991.
8. King and Schneider, op. cit.

Chapter III / A New Tool for the Reeducation of Love
1. *Vida Pitagórica*, by Jámblico, Etnos S/A, 1991.
2. *Gurdjieff: Making a New World*, by John G. Bennett, Turnstone Books, London, 1976.
3. *For Your Own Good: Hidden Cruelty in Child-Rearing and the Roots of Violence*, by Alice Miller, Farrar, Strauss, Giroux, New York, 1983.
4. Hoffman, op. cit.
5. Miller, op. cit.
6. *The Language of Psychoanalysis,* by J. Laplanche & J. B. Pontalis (Donald Nicholson-Smith translation), W. W. Norton & Co., Inc., New York, 1973 (1967).

Chapter IV / A New Shamanism for Old Adam's Problems
1. *The Shaman's Doorway: Opening Imagination to Power & Myth*, by Stephen Larsen, Station Hill Press, Barrytown, NY, 1988.
2. Brown, op. cit.
3. United Nations Conference on Trade and Development Interdependence of problems of trade, development, finance and the international monetary system; report by the Secretary-General. Geneva, UNCTAD, 6 July 1973, TD/B//459, para. 1–3.
4. Jon Tinker. "The Green Revolution is Over." New Scientist, 7 November 1974, pp. 388–393.
5. Commentary by The Club of Rome Executive Committee on The Limits to Growth. Universe Books, New York, 1973, p. 193.
6. AAAS symposium, Boston, 1969.
7. R. A. Cellarius and Joh Platt, Councils of Urgent Studies. *Science,* 25 August 1972, pp. 670–676.

8. H. Kahn and J. Wiener. "Faustian powers and human choices." In W. R. Ewald, Jr. (Ed). *Environment and Change*. Indiana University Press, Bloomington, 1968.

9. *Le Chamanisme et les Techniques Archaiques de L'Extase*, by Mircea Eliade, Payot, Paris, 1951.

10. Naranjo, op. cit.

11. *Civilization and Its Discontents*, by Sigmund Freud, L. & Virginia Woolf at the Hogarth press [etc.], London, 1930.

12. *Kundalini*, by Gopi Krishna, Shambala, Berkeley, CA, 1971.

13. *To a Dancing God*, by Sam Keen, Harper & Row, New York, 1970.

14. *Escape from Freedom*, by Erich Fromm, Holt, Rinehart and Winston, New York, 1941.

15. *The Sane Society*, by Erich Fromm, Holt, Rinehart and Winston, New York, 1955.

16. *One Dimensional Man: Studies in the Ideology of Advanced Industrial Society*, by Herbert Marcuse, Beacon Press, Boston, MA, 1964, 1968.

17. *Hallucinogens & Shamanism*, by Claudio Naranjo, edited by Michael J. Harner, Oxford University Press, New York, 1973.

About the Author

CLAUDIO NARANJO studied medicine, music, and philosophy in Chile and became known in the U.S. as one of the early staff members at Esalen Institute. A research associate at the Institute of Personality Assessment and Research (IPAR) at the Berkeley campus of the University of California, he later taught comparative religion at the California Institute of Asian Studies, and was the founder of SAT Institute, an integrative psychospiritual school devoted to holistic education.

He was a member of the Futures Planning Council of the (Episcopal) Diocese of California, has been a Fellow of the Institute of Cultural Research in London, member of the U.S. Association for The Club of Rome, member of the editorial board of *The Journal of Humanistic Psychology* during the last twenty years, is honorary president of two gestalt institutes, and has been a keynote speaker at various national and international gestalt and humanistic psychology conferences.

During the last ten years he has been most active in training psychotherapists and educators in various Latin countries.

Among his recent books in print are *How to Be* (distributed by Gateways), *Ennea-type Structures* (Gateways, 1991), *Gestalt Therapy/Attitude and Practice of an Atheoretical Experientialism* (Gateways, 1993), *Gestalt sin Fronteras* (Era Naciente, Argentina, 1993), *La Agonía del Patriarcado* (Kairós, Spain, 1993), *El Niño Divino y el Héroe* (Ed. Sirio, Spain, 1994), *Character and Neurosis/An Integrative View* (Gateways, 1994), and *Males del Mundo, Males del Alma* (*The World Problematique and the Love Crisis*) (forthcoming, Planeta, Spain).

The Earth, Totila Albert